Roses and Thorns

Beauty, Bite and Bitter Laughter

Dr. Mukesh Aseemit

Dedication

To my family -
for being the roots that ground me and the wings that lift me.

To my friends -
for their laughter in my roses and their silence through my thorns.

And to my readers and followers -
who find meaning in my satire, courage in my honesty, and joy in my words.
You make the ink flow and the thorns worth bearing

Contents

To update the Table of Contents, please right-click the field and choose'Update Field' and 'Update Entire Table.' When you update the Contents field, the fonts would automatically change to the default 'Calibri' setting given by Word. You can manually select the text and change the font to 'Gandhi serif.' Please delete these instructions once you update the Table of Contents. For more details, please go through the Reference Guide.

Foreword

I have followed Aseemit's entire body of work with great enthusiasm and curiosity. His passion for innovation-for trying something new, writing in new ways, exploring fresh subjects, and embracing learning with an almost obsessive zeal-is truly remarkable. Whether it is essays, travelogues, short stories, poetry, satire, or his active presence on social media, he continues to experiment across formats. That he does all this while being a practicing and busy doctor only adds to the wonder.

His talent is beyond question.

What makes this book even more impressive is that he has translated his own satirical Hindi writings into English-so seamlessly, in fact, that one feels as though they were originally conceived in English. In doing so, he has proven himself to be a gifted translator as well. His translations retain the spirit, flavor, and subtle charm of the original language, instantly engaging the reader. Selected Hindi satires, rendered by him into English, emerge even more vivid and compelling.
This collection strongly represents the satire being written today by the emerging generation of Hindi satirists. It brings forth the strengths and vulnerabilities of contemporary Hindi satire in all their nuances.

- Dr. Gyan Chaturvedi

Preface

From the Author

Dear Reader,

Allow me to extend a warm handshake, a knowing smirk, and a cautious warning—because what you're about to read may tickle your brain, tug at your conscience, and occasionally poke you in the ribs (purely metaphorically, of course). Roses and Thorns is my humble, and perhaps slightly audacious, attempt to plant the first full-fledged satirical flowerbed in English—grown in Indian soil, nurtured with desi manure, and trimmed with the scissors of sarcasm.

Yes, you heard that right. As far as I know, no one in India has dared—or cared enough—to publish a complete collection of satirical writings in English, at least not in a way that bridges Indian realities with universal absurdities. I am no Shakespeare of satire, nor an Orwell of irony, but I am certainly a bone doctor who has seen society limp on crutches of hypocrisy and yet dance merrily on platforms of pretense. And so, I write.

This is my first collection of English satire, and like any overenthusiastic parent of a first-born book, I am both proud and petrified. Proud, because these pages are honest; petrified, because you, dear reader, are honest too.

Within this collection, you'll meet a suspiciously secretive buffalo, a bitter gourd that deserves a literary award, a generation drowning in coaching classes, and public figures obsessed with seeing their faces in print. Each piece peels off the glossy label on our 'modernity' and reveals the hilarious, sometimes heartbreaking, truth beneath. Some stories are drawn from my experiences as a doctor, others from my misadventures as a citizen, and many more from my utterly shameless curiosity about why we behave the way we do.

I have taken the liberty to exaggerate, twist, and dramatize—but only just enough to show you what already exists. The roses in this book may smell sweet, but the thorns will make you wince with recognition.

Whether this book is successful in its mission—I leave that to you. If you chuckle, pause, reflect, or even scowl while reading, I will consider my job done. Satire, after all, is not about solutions; it's about showing the mirror, even if the mirror is cracked and the viewer slightly cross-eyed.

So, here it is—Roses and Thorns. Yours to read, to enjoy, to frown at, or to fling (preferably at someone deserving). This book is not just a collection of essays—it is an invitation to laugh at the world, and maybe, at ourselves.

With wit, warmth, and just a dash of wickedness,

Dr. Mukesh Aseemit

(Orthopedic by profession, satirist by obsession)

Acknowledgments

Writing a book is a solitary pursuit... until it isn't.

This collection wouldn't have been possible without the invisible scaffolding of support, sacrifice, and silent suffering around me. First and foremost, my heartfelt thanks to my family—my parents, who planted the seeds of literary curiosity in me; my wife, who patiently tolerated my not-so-patient writing phases, lukewarm teas, and many missed family outings (sometimes, she even pretended to read my drafts—God bless her acting skills); and my children, who accepted a temporarily absent father in exchange for permanently present books.

A warm embrace of gratitude goes out to my friends and, interestingly, my patients, who—by being patient—allowed me enough time to scribble, scratch out, and sculpt these satirical pieces between surgeries and schedules. You may not realize it, but a waiting room can be a writer's best incubator.

My sincere thanks to Jotting Press, who offered me this publishing platform—not just as a business venture, but as a literary companion that believed in satire when many considered it extinct.

To all my mentors, writers, and guiding lights who shaped this journey—I fold my hands in gratitude. A special thanks to Dr. Gyan Sir, who taught me the ABCD of satire with the seriousness of a surgeon and the mischief of a poet. To the ever-inspiring Suresh Kant ji, whose wisdom and constant encouragement made this journey bearable and beautiful.

There are thousands of unnamed well-wishers—if I begin naming them all, this acknowledgment would turn into a novella. Consider this my collective bow.

And finally, dear reader—yes, you holding this book—thank you. Your decision to pick up Roses and Thorns, and maybe even read it, is the wind beneath my writing wings. I await your reactions (and corrections!) with hopeful humility.

With gratitude and a grin,

Dr. Mukesh Aseemit

Lift the Veil, O Friend!

I am one of those overly enthusiastic friendship lovers, eager to hit my 5K target on Facebook as soon as possible—just so my page can proudly wear the "Public Figure" badge. Honestly, it gives me a bit of a celebrity-like feeling. Perhaps, Facebook's sniffing algorithms have picked up on my desperate aspirations. These days, artificial intelligence is not just intelligent; it's nosy too. It first sniffs out your feelings before deciding how to toy with them.

Earlier, I used to enjoy getting tagged in posts. My "tag-happy" friends would religiously mark me in at least ten pictures daily. My entire timeline was flooded with honeymoon snapshots, anniversary celebrations, philosophical ramblings (both wise and utterly nonsensical), and photos of gods, demons, celestial beings, and whatnot. Then, one fine day, I discovered the magic of Facebook settings! A few clicks here and there, and voila— no more unwanted tagging!

But just as I breathed a sigh of relief, Facebook, with its hyper-sensitive antennae, sniffed out my next desperate desire—to fill up my half-empty friend list! An incomplete friend list is like an underrfilled bucket—it just spills over, doesn't it?(An emty vessel makes much noise you know)) And spill over it did, as friend requests began pouring in like marriage proposals in a matrimonial ad.

The moment I clicked on a request to check out the "bride," I found—lo and behold!—a locked profile. The prospective friends were trapped behind a digital veil, eager to form a sacred bond of online friendship. But tell me, dear friends, how can a "bride-viewing ceremony" be conducted through a veil? At least let the wedding take place first; then we'll have the "lifting-the-veil" ritual!

Curious, I turned to Facebook's Help section, hoping to find some guidelines on unveiling these digital damsels before committing to friendship. No luck! The situation reminded me of those old Bollywood movies where the suhaag raat (wedding night) scene was symbolically conveyed by two flowers gently bumping into each other. Here too, the eager Facebookers who longed for my friendship had strategically placed marigold flowers, goddess idols, or "Good Morning" quotes as their display pictures. Now, was this a test of my detective skills?

For a fleeting moment, paranoia struck me—could this be my wife's undercover profile? What if I fell into a "honey trap" and my peaceful old age turned into a nightmare?

More than once, I have fallen for a charming DP and innocently accepted a friend request, only to be bombarded with messages faster than I could blink! Some of these "new friends" were more interested in my female friend list than in me. Instead of replying to my polite "Welcome to my friend list," they'd immediately dive into scanning my connections. I've since placed my friend list under lock and key—one cannot trust the wicked gaze of social media predators. Who knows when some desperate wolf might spill their filth all over my timeline? And let's not forget Facebook's moral police—one wrong word, and BAM! You're blocked.

So, to all the veil-clad brides of Facebook, I have but one humble request—

The era of veils is over! Lift the curtain, my friend!

No one falls in love with a mystery. If you wish to step into the battlefield of social media, do it with an open face. And if you're hiding something you don't want the world to see, I can recommend a sure-shot cure—every day, my newspaper delivers at least two or three magical ads claiming to fix all weaknesses. They're lying around in my veranda, waiting for you!

And here's a little poetic satire for all those locked-profile Facebookers—

To all the lovers,

The hopeless flirts, the jobless drifters—

Have you no shame?

Locking your profiles on Facebook,

Like a blushing bride behind a veil?

O darling, before sending me a friend request,

At least show me your face—

Let our eyes meet, just once!

The Pandemic of Publicity Fever

A new epidemic has spread across the nation like wildfire. In fact, ever since COVID, it seems the virus left behind a lasting imprint. This affliction is called "Chhapas"—the obsessive urge to see one's name, face, or deeds in print. Everyone is either getting published or paying to be published. Even the ED (Enforcement Directorate) and CBI (Central Bureau of Investigation) seem to be in cahoots with the media, always in search of the next sensational "chhapas-worthy" case. After all, breaking news needs a compelling "chhapas."

The way ED and CBI pursue their targets is no less than the meticulous scouting of a prospective groom's family looking for a bride. They show up unannounced, like those uninvited guests who arrive just in time for dinner. One politician, completely uninterested in chhapas, rejected their summons six times. However, when the seventh summons arrived, either due to poor eyesight or a faulty perspective, he mistook it for an "honorary invitation" and gleefully presented himself at their doorstep. Honestly, these summonses should be categorized as "letters of honor." Naturally, he was received with all the warmth and hospitality of a "damaad" (son-in-law).

Now, the politician enjoys free accommodation at his new in-laws' place, basking in the headlines daily. His body rests comfortably in the cozy quarters of his "sasural" (CBI custody), while his soul roams the corridors of newsrooms, knocking on every editor's door: "Print me! Print me!"

There are countless ways to get featured. Some prefer posters, others opt for banners. One of my friends is so obsessed with chhapas that he joins organizations just to get published. He bribes journalists with lavish treats, ensuring that in every group photo, his face shines the brightest.

Such people are born with a chhapas gene. At weddings, they plant themselves next to the groom, ensuring that they feature in every single album photo. Whether it's a wedding, funeral, or terahvi (the 13th-day mourning ritual), they insert their faces into every frame. During a photo op, they freeze in an expression of stoic enlightenment, their half-closed eyes mimicking a divine transcendence. Once the camera flash goes off, someone has to bring them back to reality.

If by chance they become a committee member, the organization is practically forced to ensure that only their photos make it to the newspapers. And when their tenure ends, they pivot to becoming an event anchor—because the itch of chhapas must be scratched at any cost.

These days, chhapas fever has infiltrated the literary world too. As the saying goes, "Do good and let it go to waste," but for these writers, the mantra is: "Write and send it to get published." They collect editors' phone numbers and email IDs like kids collect Pokémon cards, flooding inboxes with desperate pleas to get their pieces printed.

The moment their work gets published, their faces light up with the glow of a conqueror. They proudly clip their newspaper cuttings, post them all over social media, and won't rest until they've tagged at least a hundred people.

Even question papers suffer from chhapas fever! The moment they are created, they yearn to be printed. Thank goodness the printing machines refuse, insisting, "Leak first, print later!"

Politicians, of course, thrive on chhapas. During elections, their addiction to publicity becomes so severe that newspapers start resembling photo albums. They plead, "Get this published in the paper!" with the same urgency as a drowning man grasping for a life jacket.

Everything—animate, inanimate, conscious, unconscious—is infected with chhapas fever. The monsoon, too, indulges in it by flooding cities, collapsing bridges, and turning roads into rivers, ensuring its destruction makes headlines.

The common man is no different. To make it to the news, he might have to get trampled in a crowd.

Government departments are also happily bathing in the holy Ganges of chhapas, but their version involves printing stacks of currency notes. One department, however, has truly mastered "chhapas"—the police. Their motto? "First, trap them; then, print them." But they prefer printing money over making headlines. Their only fear? Getting printed in the newspapers themselves!

Publishers are churning out prints like factory assembly lines. They always manage to find a soul tormented by chhapas fever. Be it through faith, finance, or fraternity, they get their magazines printed and grant salvation to the restless writer's soul.

Politicians even get chhapas imprinted on their own faces—literally. If one cheek gets slapped, they turn the other, not out of humility, but because they want chhapas in both angles! And once they get a taste of publicity, they become chameleons, changing colors to get printed in every possible hue.

The other day, my neighbor's house was raided by the Income Tax Department. The entire town was abuzz with the news. His son's wedding prospects, which had been in limbo for ten years, suddenly skyrocketed. The moment word got out about the raid, proposals started pouring in. By the time the tax officers left, he had earned more from his son's arranged marriage than the tax department had confiscated!

Everyone is chasing chhapas. Some print currency, others print fake news. Some indulge in "chhapas" by publishing headlines, while others orchestrate raids just to make it to the front page. A few take "printing money" too literally and contribute to the flourishing counterfeit currency industry.

Even I am infected with this fever. I'm sending this piece to the editors, hoping for my own moment in print. After all, if everyone else is feasting at the chhapas buffet, why should I be left behind? I just pray that when I finally receive the editor's email, it doesn't contain their infamous catchphrase:

"We regret to inform you that we will not be publishing your work."

And before I sign off, here's an anonymous couplet—feel free to call it Ghalib's if you like:

इंसान को इंसान की ही साख मार देती है, बहुतेरों को अखबार की छपास मार देती है!
"Man kills man to maintain his reputation,"
"But many die just to make it to publication."

Bitter Gourd Juice

"Listen, I've made some bitter gourd juice, drink it before you leave!"

Just as I stepped out for my morning walk, my wife's voice echoed from behind. My cleverness had failed me yet again. Usually, my wife and I go for morning walks together, which makes escaping this bitter torment nearly impossible. But today, her legs had given up, and she decided to skip the walk.

Now, every third day, my legs too develop a rebellious streak, but I can't afford to rebel—morning walks are non-negotiable because I have adopted diabetes. Or rather, let's say diabetes is like a co-wife living in a live-in relationship with my wife. My wife, on her part, considers my body as her in-laws' house and is hell-bent on throwing this co-wife out. If only diabetes could be driven away with rolling pins or a barrage of my wife's scolding, life would have been easier. But since that's impossible, every home remedy, traditional trick, and unverified cure recommended by every self-proclaimed expert gets tested on me. And among all these, the one that has stuck to my fate like Angad's foot is—bitter gourd juice!

But today, I was overjoyed. "At least for today, I am free from bitter gourd juice!" I thought. My wife, with her aching legs, wouldn't even be able to get up from the bed! I rushed to freshen up, laced up my shoes in record time, and was about to dash out when that dreaded voice stopped me in my tracks.

Despite her "incapacitated" legs, my wife had sacrificed her deep slumber and was now dragging herself around the kitchen, preparing my beloved bitter gourd juice.

"May God never grant anyone diabetes! And if He must, at least let the wife never find out. And if the wife finds out, may the wretched friends never know!"

I swear, these so-called friends recommend such remedies—as if they are settling some ancient vendetta against me. This bitter gourd juice was also the brainchild of one such dear friend, who convinced my wife so thoroughly that now, every time I express a desire to drink something, she hands me a glass of this green torture.

"Darling, what beautiful weather today! I feel like having a drink."

And like pouring water over my excitement, she serves me bitter gourd juice, garnished with neem leaves for extra bitterness. "Cheers!"

Not just juice—bitter gourd pickle, bitter gourd curry—my entire life has turned bitter-gourd-ified!

That traitorous friend even suggested that chewing fresh neem leaves along with the juice would enhance its benefits. In frustration, I had retorted, "Brother, why not just grow bitter gourds on neem trees? That way, both remedies would merge into one!" But my wife had already made up her mind. Now, every bitter gourd juice serving comes with a topping of neem leaves.

Even the vegetable vendors recognize my wife now. The moment she steps into the market, they sprinkle water on their wilted bitter gourds to freshen them up and call out, "Madam, fresh bitter gourds today, just for you!"

One morning, as I was about to leave for my walk, I saw my wife looking dejected.

"What happened? No bitter gourd juice today?" I asked cautiously.

"The market is out of bitter gourds. The season is over," she sighed.

I had just started rejoicing when fate, not able to tolerate my happiness, whispered a brilliant idea into my wife's ears. She immediately called up my dear friend's wife.

"Bhabhi, do you have any bitter gourds at home? Need to make juice for him."

The friend's wife checked the fridge and replied, "There's one, but it's been lying there for ages, dried up like an orphan."

And just like that, my wife had my clinic staff rush over to retrieve that ancient relic, extracting every last drop of its soul to prepare half a glass of juice.

But my wife wasn't one to sit idle. Her mind spent the whole day contemplating a solution. And then, one of those wicked shopkeepers, who seem to enjoy the suffering of people like me, introduced her to bitter gourd powder—the perfect way to ensure a year-round supply!

Thus, my life truly turned as bitter as a bitter gourd.

In the parallel universe of alternative medicine, they say every ailment has a cure through opposites—if you have cold, consume heat-inducing foods; if you feel hot, consume cooling ones. Following that logic, if you have a disease caused by excess sweetness (diabetes), just drown yourself in bitterness! And so, bitter gourd and diabetes have become inseparable soulmates.

And now, here comes my wife, smiling triumphantly, holding a glass of bitter gourd juice in one hand and a glass of water in the other.

As a child, after swallowing a bitter pill, at least my mother would let me have a pinch of sugar. But here, even that mercy is denied.

So, dear reader, while I gulp down this green poison, at least spare a smile for my misfortune!

The Bachelor Son, the Miserable Father

"When someone storms into your clinic without an appointment or a slip, there's a high chance they're an acquaintance. And if they follow it up with 'Recognize me?' then you can be sure you're in for an extended, unsolicited interaction."

Sitting in my OPD, deeply engaged in my daily routine of fixing broken bones and aligning joints, I was met with an unannounced visitor. The loud, unapologetic entrance, paired with the aforementioned line, was enough to make me realize this was no ordinary patient but someone who considered their social familiarity a valid replacement for medical protocol.

From experience, I knew their real purpose wasn't treatment. They would first demand tea, then regale me with unnecessary chatter, throw in a few sarcastic jabs, and finally, as an afterthought, narrate their 'health issue.' Whatever prescription I handed them would eventually be crumpled and stuffed into their pocket with such disdain that it would remind me of my 'real place' in their hierarchy of acquaintances.

Anyway, I was used to such encounters. I played along, recognizing him quickly and ordering tea to expedite his departure. In a moment of misjudgment, I casually asked, "Uncle, what's your son up to these days? Must be married by now, right?"

The effect was instant. His expression changed, his hands gripped the chair tighter, his eyes narrowed, and as he removed his glasses to wipe them, I suspected he was dabbing away a few tears. Offering him water to replenish the sudden loss of bodily fluids seemed like the only polite thing to do.

With a deep sigh, he lamented, "What times we live in! By God's grace, we have everything—reputation, wealth. My elder daughter is married well, my son has a great job in Bengaluru, but my younger son…35 now, runs our family business, but we can't find a match for him! He's rejected ten proposals. And now, for the past five years, no new ones are even coming in! Our so-called well-wishers? They seem more intent on ensuring we never get a match than actually helping us!"

I knew his type well. A man who spent his life organizing community marriage events, matching prospective brides and grooms, delivering grand speeches on traditional values. Yet, here he was, unable to arrange his own son's wedding.

Finally, with desperation evident in his eyes, he muttered, "Doctor, if you know any girl…even a widow or divorcee, we're open to it. He's overaged now…what else can we do?"

I almost chuckled at the irony. This was the same man who had advocated for the boycott of inter-caste marriages, judged others for their 'compromised' unions, and now, he himself was contemplating the very alternative he once ridiculed.

By then, the tea had arrived. He took a sip, composed himself, and stood up to leave. It was only as he reached the door that I realized—he hadn't even mentioned a medical problem. Out of courtesy, I asked, "Uncle, what about your health?"

He sighed and waved it off, "Oh, nothing serious, I just came to see you."

And with that, he walked out, leaving behind a room full of irony.

The Summon Has Arrived

Delhi Has Called

The summon has arrived; Delhi is calling! Every eye is fixed on Delhi. Be it politicians, writers, or artists—everyone dreams of making it big in Delhi. Just like a restless lover wandering in the streets, ready to pack up and leave at the slightest beckoning from Delhi. Some rush for a rally, some for a protest, some for a ticket, some for an award—ultimately, all roads lead to Delhi! The one and only destination... The last hope of the defeated… "Chalo Dilli!"

Delhi is not just a city; it's a dream, a magnet, a benchmark, and—mind you—a washing machine, where all stains, no matter how stubborn, are washed away!

For politicians, one foot is in their constituency, the other firmly planted in Delhi. Some never even get the summon, yet they show up in Delhi every other day—perhaps hoping the summoner just forgot to call! The mere mention of a Delhi call is enough to rob them of sleep—whether they are already in power or still fighting for the throne. One loses sleep out of fear, another out of excitement. Every eye, every ear, every nerve is tuned to Delhi.

Delhi is a magician, holding every sense of every politician in its grip. Some people take a dip in the Ganges to wash away their sins, while Delhi's Yamuna is tirelessly scrubbing the sins of Delhiwalas, growing filthier by the day.

Delhi is a cloud—a swirling mass of hopes and aspirations. And when it pours, it floods fortunes. Countless moons are hidden behind these clouds, while the people back home wait for them to shine through, yearning for their return. The voters, much like a fasting wife awaiting the sight of the moon, sit hungry and veiled in hope. But Delhi's clouds, my friend... they are unpredictable!

Just as a horse never runs beyond the mosque a politician's race never goes beyond Delhi. Even our region's weather is on lease from Delhi. If a cold wave sweeps Delhi we freeze. If Delhi's temperature rises, we burn. If Delhi sneezes we run a fever of 100 degrees.

One sneeze from Delhi can bring the Sensex to its knees! Delhi is the supreme deity, and from its sanctum emerge souls that inhabit the bodies of our five-elemental leaders. These leaders' souls are already imprisoned in Delhi; only their bodies remain outside. Once elections are over, even those bodies merge into the five elements of Delhi—disappearing for five years straight.

Then comes election season—the souls start releasing from Delhi, floating back into their constituencies. The marketplace buzzes as new tenders are raised for political souls. Sold-out souls find new bodies, new avatars, new parties. These wandering spirits hunt for a new home—ministries, commissions, committees, plush offices. Meanwhile, the public remains behind, wailing like grieving families.

Politics is a cycle—what goes around, comes around. One leader goes; another takes his place. No one knows when your dreamy-eyed candidate might elope with your votes, fleeing to Delhi with your trust.

They claim, "Delhi is our father's property." Say what you will! In the end, Delhi proves time and again—it's not your father's; it's everyone's father!

This is a grand political theatre. The stage is set, the puppets are performing, and Delhi holds the strings. Delhi is the master puppeteer, pulling the strings at will—deciding who will dance, who will trip, who will be dragged down, and who will deliver the knockout punch. This game is unpredictable. The puppets change, but the play goes on. The curtain never falls—only the actors get replaced.

A politician's destiny is visible from his very first steps. Watch closely—if his feet twitch in Delhi's direction, consider his training well underway. A pilgrimage to Delhi can patch up even the most tattered kurta! A trip to Delhi is a trump card, an announcement to the world—"I've arrived!"

Just as an NRI returnee commands special respect in society, a Delhi-return politician enjoys unparalleled prestige. That tag alone skyrockets his market value! Once he's Delhi-return, he's showroom material—fit to be displayed with pride.

And oh, the Delhi-return tail! Once acquired, it becomes a badge of honor, a fly-swatter against all nuisances. It's not just a tail; it's an official Delhi stamp!

Delhi is contagious. Those who visit bring back as much of Delhi as they can carry. Delhi seeps into their souls, its arrogance fuels their power, and its connections smoothen the impossible. Many impossible tasks are done simply by flashing the Delhi-eye!

There are two kinds of Delhi-returns—one who's actually called, and another who goes uninvited but markets it as a special summon. Come election season, Delhi overflows with these eager pilgrims, all desperately vying for a ticket—even if they must buy it on the black market.

Schemes, camps, factions, lobbying, sama-dama-danda-bhed—all in pursuit of one wish, one ambition: "This time, may Delhi call us in!"

Chandumal just returned from Delhi. His disciples are pampering him, yet he looks dejected. Perhaps, fate's bounty did not spill into his courtyard. Despite all efforts, his longtime rival—who once rode as a backseat passenger in his Delhi-bound car—has now bought his own vehicle and zoomed past him. He left before Chandumal even got wind of it.

Chandumal stares blankly at his chair. It seems shaky. A sinking heart, a storm of worries.

"What happened? Why was I called? The party is under fire—why am I being made the scapegoat? Are they about to demand my resignation?"

So many uncertainties!

Ah, Delhi and the Delhi-returns! Blessed be your fate!

Chinta Camp (Worry Workshop)

This morning, my neighbor, Sharma Ji, barged into my house. He had come to return my newspaper, which he had conveniently "borrowed" earlier. Along with it, he also brought a leaflet that had fallen out. These leaflets always seem to find their way to me. Sharma Ji is a dutiful neighbor—he kidnaps my newspaper, reads it first, and then delivers the news to me in person, all while enjoying a cup of tea at my expense. At home, his wife only gives him plain tea, so he makes sure to enjoy the sweet one here.

Anyway, let's get to the point. Today, Sharma Ji was holding a leaflet and said, "You never read the newspaper, at least look at the pamphlets inside. A very important event is happening in our city."

I replied, "What now? Another showroom opening? A new restaurant? A coaching center? Some herbal doctor claiming to cure all skin diseases? A de-addiction camp? A love guru promising to turn failed relationships into success stories? Or a doctor's visiting schedule?"

Sharma Ji said, "No, Garg Sahab! This is different. A famous spiritual guru, Chintamani Baba, is organizing a 'Worry Workshop' in town!"

I was taken aback. "A worry workshop?" The leaflet looked so fancy that even it seemed worried about how to best spread worry among people. A bold tagline caught my eye—"Show your worries, get in the limelight!"

"I've heard of meditation camps and self-reflection retreats, but what on earth is a worry workshop?" I asked.

Sharma Ji enthusiastically explained, "Garg Sahab, worrying is essential these days. How else will you run your household? Even governments survive by worrying! Just watch TV debates, political rallies, or intellectual discussions—everywhere, you'll find people deep in worry. But you, you don't worry enough! Worrying is an art, and it must be learned. I am definitely attending this workshop. If you want, let me know."

I quickly sent him on his way but sat there for a while, genuinely worried about this whole 'worry' business. Sharma Ji wasn't wrong—everyone in this country is busy worrying, but no one is actually doing any work. Worry is everywhere. Politicians worry in their speeches, during election campaigns, even when going door-to-door. They express their concerns in parliament, fume with anger over issues, organize protests, and even curse others—all out of 'worry.' Strikes, protests, and hunger strikes are all born out of worry.

The government worries about water, electricity, and the poor. The opposition worries that the government doesn't worry enough. A bridge collapses—worry. The government falls— worry. The currency falls—worry. The common man? He has no time to worry about the country; he's too busy worrying about whether his family will get their next meal. So, politicians and policymakers take on the noble responsibility of worrying on his behalf.

Even globally, worry is a powerful force. One country worries about human rights in another and launches an attack. Another worries about climate change and imposes restrictions on others.

I have a friend who is a government clerk. He has mastered the art of worrying. His strategy is simple—never work, just worry about work. Every morning, he arrives at the office and sits in front of his boss with a deeply concerned expression, worrying about pending files. He even brings home his boss's personal worries, adding them to his own collection. His boss, relieved to share his worries, feels much lighter.

Politicians and their followers move in groups, collectively wearing their 'worried' expressions. The leader sheds crocodile tears, and the public is expected to drown in them. They say, "Worry is like a funeral pyre." Indeed, the politicians worry, and the public suffers the consequences.

I know Sharma Ji well—he keeps upgrading his worrying skills. His face carries a permanent expression of distress. The moment he steps into his house, he looks so troubled that his wife rushes to get him water, assuming something terrible has happened. He once made the mistake of entering the house with a smile. His wife immediately suspected something fishy—"Why are you so happy today? Met your old flame at the market, didn't you?" That day, the house turned into a battlefield. Since then, he has vowed never to enter his home with a cheerful face.

Now, he's planning to attend this worry workshop. Looks like he is preparing for his post-retirement career in politics. After all, worry is the lifeblood of leaders, and Sharma Ji seems to be getting ready in advance.

In every corner of society, people are trapped in a cycle of worry. Politicians worry about the nation but worry even more about their election victories. Intellectuals worry about society but are more concerned about their Twitter engagement. Religious leaders worry about the world's sins but are more focused on increasing their follower count.

Worry is no longer genuine; it has become a staged performance. Politicians, religious figures, and social leaders have turned it into a thriving business. And people like Sharma Ji? They just want to learn new techniques to perfect their 'worried' expressions—so that when someone looks at them, they immediately believe that this man carries the burden of the entire world on his shoulders.

Imitation Ain't Easy!

Imitation, too, requires intelligence. Yet, people are so terrified of it that warnings are plastered everywhere— "Beware of Imitators!" Ever since the democratic constitution introduced the concept of copyright, people have interpreted it in their own ingenious ways. Every law is like a chameleon—you twist it as per your convenience. That's precisely why laws exist: so that you can interpret them to your advantage. Without someone to lean on, poor law just wanders around like an orphan.

And supporting orphans is a noble act, isn't it? Take the copyright law, for instance. No matter how much legal experts yell their lungs out explaining it, we've settled on its real meaning— "The Right to Copy!" Meaning, copying is our fundamental right. After all, interpreting laws correctly adds meaning to life, makes them economically viable, and, of course, contributes to the ever-declining national economy.

Don't underestimate imitation— call it jugaad instead! It is a national art form, flourishing in every nook and corner of India. As kids, cheating in exams was an unwritten part of our curriculum. The golden rule? Use what's already written instead of troubling your brain! And as we grew up, we diligently applied this divine skill in every aspect of life.

Take government schemes, for example. The moment a new policy is introduced, a brigade of "experts" activates. Be it forging documents for subsidies, securing loans, manufacturing fake passports, Aadhaar cards, or ration cards—everything is conjured up in a jiffy, with such finesse that even investigative agencies might discard the real one as fake, while the fake appears more authentic than the original!

Once, my wife asked me to get some namkeen from a famous shop— Shankar Namkeen Bhandar. Now, I'm a rookie when it comes to shopping, but the wife's command is the wife's command. Off I went, bag in hand! (No, not wearing a bag, don't get me wrong!).

The market greeted me with twenty identical shops— Shiv Shankar, Jai Shankar, Bhole Shankar, Maha Shankar, Jai Shiv Shankar! There were four shops named Shankar Namkeen alone! I was utterly bewildered.

Upon calling my wife for guidance, she replied, "Buy from the shop with the longest queue." Now, being a time-efficient person, I applied reverse logic—I picked the shop with the shortest queue!

Namkeen is namkeen, after all! And let's be honest, does anything "authentic" even digest in our stomachs anymore? Chemical-laced milk, synthetic paneer, spices laced with cow dung, rice and lentils mixed with pebbles—our digestive systems have turned into fortresses, impervious to anything remotely organic.

Many businesses thrive solely on this imitation industry. In some states, it's even granted organized sector status! Every now and then, newspapers flash pictures of students dangling from windows in exam centers, an undeniable testament to this industry's national significance.

Imitation also serves as a great equalizer, putting a check on monopolistic brand owners. The copy-paste culture on social media is a spectacle in itself! At times, it feels like Mark Zuckerberg personally bestowed some people the divine right to copy content and slap their names on it!

Yet, some people remain benevolent—rather than attributing stolen poetry to themselves, they kindly credit Ghalib, as if Ghalib was the original heir to every anonymous verse on the internet!

Copycats are always on high alert—ears perked, eyes wide open, noses sniffing for the next golden opportunity. Once they snag the loot, they proudly post it on Facebook, distributing it "for the greater good"—a modern interpretation of "Charity begins on social media."

And let's get one thing straight— you're only a thief if you steal and keep it to yourself. But if you share it openly, people will worship you, forwarding your content with folded hands, chanting praises like devotees at a temple!

Take our town's poet, Kavi Kulshreshth. He prefers the title "Beloved Poet of the City." His poetic genius depends entirely on which poetry he has plagiarized. He effortlessly morphs into the sentiment of the stolen poem.

Ironically, while pilfering poems is a casual affair, he meticulously inspects envelopes filled with cash, ensuring no organizer dares slip in a counterfeit note!

The imitation industry is a godsend for the middle class, patching up their tattered dreams.

For the rich, Chor Bazaar (the flea market) is a mere inconvenience, but for the middle class, it's a gateway to borrowed luxury. It allows them to slip into branded shoes their budget could never afford—at least for a few glorious steps of self-deception.

Every city has a Chor Bazaar. Even if it doesn't sell stolen goods, it certainly sells top-notch knock-offs. You name it—TVs, shoes, washing machines, clothes—just pick your brand, and voila! The logo is printed right there for you.

The result? Happy family, happier neighbors!

"Oh, you must visit! We just got a brand-new 42-inch Sony TV. Bhabhi ji, do come over—we'll watch the T20 finals together!"

Frankly, I believe "The Art of Imitation" should be introduced as a formal subject in schools. At the very least, it will help our unemployed, unskilled, and good-for-nothing youth contribute meaningfully to the systematic wreckage of the nation!

"Dreams Trapped in Coaching Classes :

A Reflection on Modern Education"

These days, social media is flooded with mark sheets, all showing above 90% scores. It seems as if no student scores below that anymore. Education policies have changed, and students now receive generous marks—nobody fails. But it wasn't always like this. Back in our time, passing board exams was rare. Out of a class of 30, only two or three would pass. If someone secured a first division, the entire village would celebrate. There would be feasts, devotional songs, and even religious gatherings!

I remember when my school was newly upgraded to the matriculation level. For the first two years, not a single student passed. The school was on the verge of being downgraded, teachers panicked, and many were transferred. The new teachers then handpicked two students and pleaded with them to pass the exams for the school's reputation. I was one of those students.

Honestly, school was never a priority for us. We worked harder to skip school than today's kids work to top their coaching classes. In our time, skipping school meant a day of fun and adventure. Today, if parents keep their children home even for a family function, they act as if their entire career is at stake!

Speaking of marks, back then, we only cared about the passing percentage—33%. Even that was sometimes achieved with grace marks. Today, students score 98%, which would have been enough to pass three students in our time! Some students stayed in the same class for years, as if they were on a five-year plan.

Teachers would retire, but these students remained. Many of them eventually became school monitors and later, politicians. After all, the foundation of leadership is laid in school!

Books were scarce, and there was no concept of a structured syllabus. The same textbooks were used for generations—first by an elder sibling, then passed down to cousins and neighbors. In English, we memorized just three things: the story of the "Thirsty Crow," a formal leave application to the headmaster, and an essay on cows. We only started learning the alphabet in sixth grade! Spelling competitions consisted of reciting basic words. It took us two years just to master "W-H-A-T, what!"

The famous cow essay was a universal template. If asked to write about school, we simply replaced "cow" with "school." The key was to fill up as many pages as possible. To impress the teacher, we would take extra answer sheets.

Since our school had a history of failing students, the teachers devised a foolproof plan for our exams. Two teachers were stationed outside to watch for inspection squads, while the rest distributed cheat sheets inside. This strategy saved our school from being downgraded.

Back then, neither parents nor students were overly concerned about careers. If, by chance, we studied late at night, our parents would say, "Go to sleep now; you can study tomorrow." Our school bags sat neglected in a corner all day and were only picked up when the school bell rang the next morning. We didn't know why, but our school bags felt like a burden. Homework was finished at school itself, and we were accustomed to teachers' scoldings and punishments. The moment a teacher entered the classroom, half the students automatically became "murga" (a common punishment where students squat with their hands through their legs).

Today, students get depressed even after scoring 99%—they question the examiner over that missing 1%. Children are thrown into competition from as early as sixth grade. Their childhood is being snatched away. Instead of toys, fairs, puppet shows, and hide-and-seek, their hands hold heavy school bags and their parents' endless expectations.

Where are the comics that shaped our childhood—Champak, Chacha Chaudhary, and Sabu? Where are those simple joys? Kids, trapped in the complex formulas of chemistry and physics, just want to breathe, but we don't notice their suffocation. Instead, we applaud their "success."

Success used to be passing an exam, but now even securing a merit position isn't enough. As soon as a child makes it to the merit list, new competitive goals are forced upon them. Coaching institutes use them as brand ambassadors, putting their faces on hoardings, draping them in garlands, and using them for marketing. The child's own dreams are lost—they are merely fulfilling their parents' ambitions or boosting a coaching institute's business.

The saddest part of today's education system is that childhood innocence, playfulness, and dreams are vanishing. Children are running in a race for marks as if they are machines designed for maximum productivity. Instead of encouraging curiosity and creativity, we burden them with assignments and entrance exam preparations.

Once, a lost child at a village fair would rush to his mother's call. Today, the same child eagerly waits to hear his roll number in a coaching center. That free-spirited childhood is lost. Kids today are like their school bags—neglected and burdened.

Education was once about gaining knowledge; now, it is merely a numbers game. Parents and teachers who once focused on values and ethics are now obsessed with career counseling and success metrics. Childhood has been reduced to a résumé, filled with certificates and merit ranks.

With increasing mental health issues and student suicides, psychiatric counseling has become more necessary than career counseling.

Perhaps, the greatest celebration in education will be the day we let children chase their own dreams, instead of forcing ours onto them.

There Goes the Buffalo…
Straight into the Water!

The political landscape of the nation was shaken to its core. Such a spectacle hadn't been witnessed even during the Emergency days—though we've only heard tales of those times when governments fell, crumbled, were rebuilt, then fell again, and the old ones came back to power.

But today was something else entirely. The entire government was under suspicion! The breaking news flashed across all channels—the government's buffalo had plopped into the water and refused to get up! The entire country was in an uproar.

TV channels tripped over each other to break the story, falling head over heels in a frenzy. Every channel was hell-bent on proving why this was indeed the biggest breaking news of the century. Opinion polls were launched—

"Will the buffalo come out or remain seated in the water?"

"What are the odds?"

"Call this hotline now to vote!"

Or simply type GOVTBUFFALO YES or NO and send it to this number.

Soon, the hashtag #GovtBuffalo was trending on Twitter. The entire nation was gripped by discussions about the government's buffalo.

Now, the government had an entire herd of buffaloes, but since this one rebelled—or perhaps sat in the water as per the government's grand plan—it was bound to go viral.

The biggest question on everyone's lips: "What exactly does this buffalo do?"

"What does it eat?"

"Which breed are government buffaloes?"

"Does it even produce dung?"

"And if it does, where does that dung go? Is the government exporting it and depositing the money in Swiss accounts?"

Theories flew left and right. The public, as always, had its mouth running at full speed. But, of course, what's the point of playing the flute before a government buffalo?

Soon, TV studios turned into battlefields of heated debates. Opposition leaders poured in statements like monsoon floods. Meanwhile, channels, lacking a fresh breaking story, continued milking this one dry.

When they couldn't locate the buffalo shed, they decided to besiege the Parliament and State Assemblies instead. And guess who led the siege? Not the opposition, not the activists—but the media itself!

Finally, using their top-secret Jaichand-grade insider sources, news channels cracked the case—they found the buffalo shed!

Hordes of reporters rushed to the scene. Microphones were shoved into the faces of every buffalo in sight. One particularly enthusiastic reporter even waded into the water, mic in hand, and went straight up to the buffalo.

"Are you in any distress?"

"Has the government held you hostage?"

"Did you willingly sit in the water, or is this part of a larger conspiracy?"

The buffalo merely shook its head, but that was enough for TV anchors to twist it into a scandalous headline.

"Did you see that, folks? The government's buffalo has spoken! The nation demands to know—does the government even own this buffalo or not?"

"Why has the government hidden its buffalo statistics from the public?"

"Stay tuned! Our fearless reporters are digging deeper into this investigation!"

Meanwhile, on another channel, an opposition spokesperson furiously demanded—

"First, let's find out why the buffalo sat in the water in the first place! This buffalo belongs to the government, so why isn't it getting up? Was it bribed with tax-free liquor?"

Yet another news channel, taking its journalistic duties seriously, ran a full-fledged documentary on buffalo lifestyle—what they eat, how they graze, how they relax. A panel of expert buffalo analysts was called in for their valuable insights.

Now, these so-called buffalo experts were in high demand, as channels scrambled to get them on air. Their fodder costs were covered as part of their guest appearance fees!

One reporter, in an attempt to prove historical precedence, reminded the nation of the Great Buffalo Fodder Scam, where the government had gulped down buffalo fodder meant for the animals.

"And today, history repeats itself!"

Buffaloes were trending on TV, and urban children were glued to their screens, watching Buffalo Darshan unfold. The media spun this into a symbol of urban-rural connectivity.

Soon, Parliament descended into chaos. The opposition accused the government of running a black-market buffalo racket.

"The government claims to raise cows, but in reality, it's been secretly nurturing buffaloes! This is a direct attack on religious sentiments!"

Demands were made for an official parliamentary inquiry.

"Are these even real buffaloes? Or are they actually cows disguised in black paint?"

"And if the government insists on raising buffaloes, why didn't they include pigs as well? After all, pigs can sit comfortably in the mud, unlike buffaloes, who need water. Given the government's ability to create a mess everywhere, pigs would've been the perfect choice!"

Finally, environmental activists entered the fray—"The country is already facing a water crisis! Wasting water just so buffaloes can sit in it is a blatant violation of the government's water policy!"

And so, the nation continued debating, investigating, and screaming about the greatest crisis of our time—THE GOVERNMENT'S BUFFALO IN THE WATER!

The Miser Extraordinaire

A recent international news headline featured a millionaire woman crowned as the world's stingiest rich person. Despite her immense wealth, she spends an astonishingly minimal amount on food and daily needs.

Now, dictionaries may define 'miserliness,' but they fail to capture the true essence of a miser. In reality, a miser's stinginess is not just a behavioral trait—it's embedded in their very DNA. If scientists were to analyze their genetic structure, they'd probably discover a "miser gene" tucked away in their chromosomes.

Generally, miserliness is associated with money-hoarding—those who collect wealth but refuse to spend it, neither enjoying it themselves nor letting others benefit. But let's not forget, these misers are far less harmful than the looters, hoarders, and loan sharks who thrive on robbing others. Misers, at least, stick to their sacred motto: "Chamdi jaye par damdi na jaye" (Let my skin peel, but not a single penny should be lost). They have upheld this philosophy through generations.

And honestly, why should anyone have a problem with their money? It's theirs to hoard, bury, or even burn—why should it bother you? In fact, thanks to such misers, treasure hunters have often stumbled upon buried riches. Some people even deliberately buy properties belonging to legendary misers, hoping to uncover hidden fortunes.

Back in my school days, there was an ancient sweet shop in our village, and I vividly remember one of our miserly old teachers. He had no children, but he was secretly a wealthy man. He lent money at interest—not against silver, but only gold! Yet, he never flaunted his riches, despite knowing that after his death, his wealth would be looted by distant relatives. He ate sweets only once a year—on Diwali. For him, Diwali wasn't about lights or celebrations; it was about desi ghee Imartis. A kilogram of those was his fixed quota, which he spent the rest of the year digesting. After all, a miser's digestive system isn't designed for luxury— God made sure of that!

Some misers are stingy only with money, but others take it a step further—they are miserly with emotions, respect, and even hospitality. You'll never hear a word against them, though. Then there's a special breed: those who spend lavishly on themselves but wouldn't spare a single coin for charity. Their philosophy? "Maya is for bhog (enjoyment), but only for oneself!"

But nature has its way of balancing things. Ironically, the offspring of such extreme misers often undergo a "genetic mutation," turning into extravagant spendthrifts. They keep an eagle eye on their father's wealth and practically loot their own homes. Such poor misers, tormented by their own children, often develop various illnesses—but they even consider their ailments as assets! Their logic? "At least something is accumulating, nothing is going waste, even if it's just diseases!"

Doctors are their worst nightmare. Rather than seeking professional treatment, they prefer bizarre home remedies suggested by neighbors. If illness becomes unavoidable, they borrow prescriptions from others and bargain at medical stores for the highest discounts. A ten-day medicine course? Nah! They'll buy just two days' worth and stretch it across five.

The funniest part? Even diseases seem to get frustrated with them and leave! While politicians spend on advertising, rallies, and donations to gain public attention, misers become the talk of the town effortlessly. They are the staple topic at every roadside tea stall, accompanying every sip of chai.

Every neighborhood has a "miser's mansion"—an infamous house everyone recognizes and avoids, whether it's donation seekers or vote-hungry politicians. It's not that they demand money for votes—God forbid! That would mean giving something, which is against their nature. They know how to earn but have never learned how to give. As a result, they don't even cast votes!

Yet, when it comes to receiving, they are unbeatable. They shamelessly queue up at community feasts and charity food distributions. During post-Diwali Annakoot feasts, you'll spot them sitting cross-legged with a banana leaf in front of them, eagerly waiting for free food. Embarrassment? Shame? What's that? They live by their miserly principles, immune to public mockery.

A particularly legendary miser family lives near my house. Their sons have not only upheld but taken their father's legacy to new heights! Even the daughters-in-law have mastered the art of miserliness. Their house is so strategically designed that they save half their electricity costs—why switch on lights when you can steal brightness from the neighbor's courtyard? Their electric meter moves slower than time itself!

Their Wi-Fi strategy? Emotional blackmail! They trick neighbors into sharing passwords by narrating sob stories about their children's education. Despite being well-off, they claim every possible government benefit designed for the poor. No sooner is a welfare scheme announced than they are the first to apply. Even their children's jobs were secured using EWS (Economically Weaker Section) certificates!

And waste? There's barely any. Even the municipal garbage collector is delighted—because they have nothing to give, not even trash!

Stray dogs and cows instinctively avoid their house. Once, they attempted an act of generosity—feeding a dog. But it wasn't out of kindness; it was because a rat had invaded their house and stolen a chapati. The entire family mourned that lost chapati like it was a national tragedy. When they finally retrieved it— half-eaten and stale—they decided to donate it to a street dog. The poor dog suffered four days of vomiting, after which the canine community collectively boycotted their house.

Even cows had a bad experience—once tricked into entering their home, milked dry, and then unceremoniously shooed away. Eventually, the cows wisened up and never returned.

Uncle and Aunty have been using the same medical prescription for the past 20 years. Whenever they fall ill, they simply pull out the old prescription and buy the same medicines. No doctor visits, no unnecessary spending—it's a mutual understanding between them and the healthcare system!

One day, during a morning walk, I casually suggested, "Now that you're free of responsibilities, why not go on a Chardham Yatra (a sacred pilgrimage)?"

He replied in a profound, philosophical tone, "Why search for God in temples when He is omnipresent? Our home itself is the Chardham!"

Every other day, Aunty or her daughters-in-law ring the neighbors' doorbells—to borrow curd, sugar, tea leaves, onions, potatoes, or even cooking oil! In summers, every household in the colony stores an extra bowl of ice just for them. But one day, their miserliness cracked, and they finally bought a fridge. The entire neighborhood celebrated the occasion!

Their transport? Always borrowed from the neighbors. Their own scooter, dating back to prehistoric times, stands in their courtyard like a museum artifact.

Their gas cylinder? Borrowed. Their water supply? Public taps.

Honestly, miserliness could be rebranded as financial prudence and introduced as a national curriculum for children. In fact, this miser family could conduct hands-on workshops on extreme money-saving techniques!

One thing is certain—misers live long lives, simply because they spend even life sparingly. And if anyone dares to criticize their lifestyle, they have a ready arsenal of philosophical answers:

Criticism: "Why live so frugally?"

Reply: "We follow Gandhi's principle: 'Simple living, high thinking'!"

Criticism: "Why don't you go to doctors when you fall sick?"

Reply: "Doctors invent diseases! Fresh air, sunlight, and warm water—God's free gifts—are the best medicine!"

So, should I wrap up this Miser Purana here? Or should I economize my words a bit more?

No Time – A Satirical Piece

In the whirlwind world of white coats and stethoscopes, there exists a phrase that has become a badge of honor, especially among us doctors: "No time." No time to die, even! Proclaiming that you have no time is the modern-day shining armor of the knights of the medical realm. If a doctor does not chant this mantra, it is an unspoken universal truth that their practice is in dire straits.

I, too, have cracked the code. When I need a break, a meal, or just some peace, I slip away with the classic excuse—"There's a case going on in the operation theater." And then? Feet up, a steaming cup of tea in hand, and a deep dive into the endless abyss of the internet.

This scene has played out countless times in my life. I sit in the OPD, patiently attending to my patients—taking my time, a practice that, I am well aware, is almost scandalous in the world of medicine. A village woman, sensing the eerie calm before the storm, eyes me suspiciously. She is baffled that I am actually taking the time to examine her properly.

"Doctor," she begins, "There's barely any crowd here."

She then narrates her experience at another doctor's clinic, which was overflowing with patients as if free prasad was being distributed at a temple. I explain to her that the other doctor probably gave her a grand total of two minutes, whereas I've spent ten minutes on her case. Clearly, I am prioritizing quality over quantity, right?

But the truth is this: Patients prefer doctors who appear to be drowning in work. It seems being busy is the ultimate seal of authenticity. The busier the doctor, the better he must be! If a doctor's chamber has only a handful of patients, it raises the same suspicion as an empty restaurant—something must be wrong.

And this extends beyond the clinic. At home, if my wife catches me idle for even a moment, she immediately starts invoking every deity we know, worrying about our livelihood. "God knows what's wrong these days! Look at so-and-so's practice, and then look at you. Are you even treating patients properly?"

Thus, I find myself trapped in the vicious cycle of "no time," sacrificing my desires at the altar of my schedule, perpetually waiting in my own clinic, wondering—this wasn't exactly the package deal I signed up for when I became a doctor! And when I got married, my in-laws certainly didn't mention a terms & conditions clause that stated I had to contract the "No Time Syndrome"!

To add salt to the wound, my colleagues often remark, "Suddenly interested in literature? Writing, huh? Must be nice to have so much free time. Yaar ..how canm you do it..here I can barely breathe with the patient load!"

For some reason, I have never quite mastered the sacred art of the "No Time" chant. I am the type who happily accepts invitations for outings, festival celebrations, or any social event—because, obviously, I "always have time." My enthusiastic participation has even led some friends and relatives to express their deep concern:

"Poor guy. These days, there are so many new orthopedic doctors in town… but don't worry, God will make things right."

Their concern would be amusing if it didn't sometimes reach the Home Ministry—a.k.a. my wife. That's when I truly realize how merciless God can be—for He has cursed me with an abundance of time!

Some people marvel at my ability to juggle multiple responsibilities, while others speculate that I must have mastered the art of time management. Some call me a multi-tasker, but their smirks betray the satisfaction they derive from having truly surrendered to this profession.

I, on the other hand, grapple with the guilt of my apparent idleness—constantly seeking philosophical justifications for my unstructured existence.

So, in a world where "No Time" is the new normal, I sit here wondering—perhaps my peculiar hobby of dusting off old passions is nothing but a silent rebellion against madness. The glamorous life of a doctor, where every second counts, and yet, ironically, time stands idly before me, waiting to be used.

Dr. Mukesh Aseemit

Numbers Speak, You See!

I was reading the newspaper when a headline made me jump in surprise. It was about an organization that had just conducted a blood donation camp. Incidentally, I had also donated blood at the same camp. At the top of the article, there was a photograph of a donor lying on a bed—someone who looked suspiciously like me—surrounded by a lively crowd of twenty people from the organization. While clicking the photo, they had been extra careful not to obscure the banner displaying the organization's name. Some members even bent at the waist to ensure the name remained visible—because priorities, you see!

But what truly made my forehead crease in suspicion was the staggering number of blood donations reported. It was four times the actual count! And just like that, it all made sense—organizations and statistics go hand in hand, like two peas in a pod. After all, these organizations thrive on bloated figures. Without such "harvests of numbers," their sacred buffaloes wouldn't produce milk. These NGOs, which are sprouting like mushrooms after the rain, sustain themselves by multiplying statistics tenfold and milking lucrative government schemes in the name of public service. They, too, understand that by the time a fund of [1] 100 reaches their hands, it has already been whittled down to [1] 25.

There's an old saying in our village: "Just keep feeding the buffaloes kans (wild grass) and the government inflated numbers, and you can milk both indefinitely." Mind you, this is no new trend—it probably started in ancient times. Even Lord Chitragupta in heaven keeps detailed numerical accounts of every living soul's deeds, which are then presented to the almighty Dharmaraj. Based on these very figures, one is assigned either to heaven or hell. And so, the practice trickled down to Earth, first adopted by government offices, bureaucracies, and schools, only to become the lifeblood of every non-governmental institution and political establishment over time.

Over the years, various artistic techniques have been devised to dress up these numbers—line charts, bar graphs, pie charts, pixel diagrams, PowerPoint slides—you name it! Financial companies, chit funds, loan providers, stock market sharks, and lottery schemes have all joined hands to prey on the ever-suffering middle class. Armed with eye-catching statistical presentations, they lure us in. And the poor middle-class man, rather than being swayed by the figures in these charts, often gets hypnotized by the curves and smiles of the glamorous women presenting them, only to be trapped in their elaborate financial web.

Meanwhile, multi-level marketing (MLM) schemes have taken statistical manipulation to another level. They mesmerize their targets with dazzling dreams, pushing them up the ladder of illusion—a classic example of what we colloquially call "chadhaa diya ped pe" (hoisting someone up a tree). Politicians, too, have cracked the code. Knowing full well that people are tired of their empty promises, they now resort to an even greater illusion—fabricated statistics! To prove their so-called progress, every department spends five years compiling impressive-looking figures, and just before elections, these carefully curated number games are unleashed upon the unsuspecting public.

Numbers rule everything—TV debates, newspaper headlines, government offices, loans, banks, universities, hospitals, municipalities, panchayats, secretariats—everywhere, it's the same tune: the symphony of statistics. Whether or not government schemes reach the grassroots level is irrelevant; what truly matters is that they appear to be flourishing on paper! Some master magicians are hard at work conjuring up numerical illusions to bolster the country's GDP. After all, it is only through such statistical bait that the consumer-fish can be reeled in.

Our own city boasts a number-crunching wizard, a political strategist whose bag of magical statistics can shake up entire elections. His graphs predict which party is sinking, who is afloat, and who's set to win. In his world, bar charts talk, percentages determine destinies, and pie charts account for every last penny.

But let's not forget the politicians themselves—they don't just dish out inflated statistics, they consume them too! Now that elections are around the corner, they're busy cooking up a lavish buffet of numerical delicacies—"development data" served with a side of rhetorical garnish. After all, the path to power is paved with statistical trickery!

Election analysts have rolled out the chessboard of numbers, and fresh-faced politicians are climbing the ladder of statistics, dreaming of victory. Ward-wise calculations are so precise that they can predict the number of votes from each caste and neighborhood with surgical accuracy. The astrological gymnastics of numbers have reached such dizzying heights that political strategists are already declaring victory even before the first vote is cast—

"Netaji, within thirty minutes of polling, your win is guaranteed! Trust us, the numbers say so!"

Statistics have conquered everything, even personal relationships! Your bank balance, your income statements—all of these figures determine how many relatives will show up for your wedding, birthday, or even your funeral.

In the end, numbers don't just speak, they scream! And as for the common man? Well, he has no choice but to hold his head and weep. Because in this great numerical game of chess, the king is always the one in power… and the people? They're just the pawns waiting to be sacrificed.

Paper Leak:
The New Business of Education and Politics

These days, one news story is "leaking" more than anything else—exam paper leaks. Almost every other day, some exam paper or the other gets leaked. When even the wheels of democracy are leaking air, how can paper leaks be a big deal? These leaks not only make headlines but also provide opportunities for the government to form inquiry committees, for ruling and opposition parties to blame each other, and for investigative agencies like the CBI and ED to conduct raids on political opponents. In short, these leaks sow the seeds for upcoming election campaigns.

Politicians have accepted that these "stains" on democracy's fabric are now part of the design. They even claim that these stains give democracy an "antique" look! The leaks are not limited to just exam papers; the entire system is leaking. Sometimes, the number of rebel MLAs gets leaked, leading to government collapses. Sometimes, a politician's scandalous video leaks, providing entertainment to the public. And sometimes, a corrupt official's bribery video leaks, exposing yet another layer of our rotten system.

When leaks are everywhere, how can exam papers be any different? If papers don't leak, how will the "business" of rigging exams survive? This is a crucial livelihood for many who ensure that doctors, engineers, and government employees keep emerging from every household. Degrees are being distributed like government freebies. The government might not be handing out jobs as freebies, but people have figured out a way to secure at least a degree. After all, even if they don't get a job, they can still enter politics without opposition taunting them about being uneducated.

Getting a degree through hard work has become nearly impossible these days. Reservation has already made things difficult, and whatever little hope remains is crushed by the skyrocketing fees of coaching centers. Private colleges charge fees as if they are swallowing students whole. So, if someone can manage a leaked paper, pay a few lakhs, and secure admission in a government college, then why not? Once they get in, they'll find a way to pass. Colleges themselves push students through, eager to get rid of them with a degree in hand.

This paper leak business has become a new fundraising method for political parties. Since the Supreme Court has put restrictions on electoral bonds, political parties are desperate for funds. Elections don't run on slogans alone—money is needed to buy MLAs and MPs, organize rallies, and distribute cash in exchange for votes. Corporate houses don't support every party equally; they choose a favorite and stick with it. Meanwhile, agencies like ED and CBI keep politicians on edge. Amidst all this, paper leaks remain a reliable source of income, though even this "business" is now under scrutiny.

Supply always follows demand. If people want leaked papers, the market will provide them. The day is not far when paper leaks will be officially legalized. Perhaps the Constitution will be amended to introduce a clause allowing people to pay a fixed fee to the government and an additional ten times that amount in bribes to secure leaked papers. Coaching centers will lose their monopoly, and a true form of socialism will emerge—one where all students, regardless of merit, will be equal. Why bother with intelligence or hard work when you can simply buy a degree?

Imagine a future where degrees are handed out like garlands at welcome ceremonies. Honorary doctorate degrees are already being sold like street food, and foreign universities are more than happy to award degrees in exchange for hefty donations. Soon, there will be home delivery for degrees!

Every new trend faces some resistance initially. Now that paper leaks have become an integral part of every competitive exam, people's faith in exams has started to fade. Coaching institutes that proudly display their toppers might soon find that people suspect those names were simply beneficiaries of leaked papers. Even genuine toppers will struggle to prove their merit.

Parents will gradually accept this as the new normal. Democracy has given us many rights, and maybe we should accept leaks as its natural byproduct. After all, when a child wets the bed, parents are initially annoyed but eventually learn to live with it. Our democracy is no different. The system is flat, but we are still dragging its broken wheels forward.

Politicians know that public memory is short. People will protest for a few days and then move on. And if they don't, a new religious controversy or riot will conveniently distract them. The public only needs entertainment; the form it takes doesn't really matter.

The students who actually work hard, whose dreams are being stolen, may take their grievances to court, filing petitions and running from pillar to post. But will it change anything? The government will simply file an affidavit promising to make future exams "leak-proof." Maybe they'll even suggest printing question papers on khadi fabric instead of paper to align with Gandhi's ideology! Perhaps they'll set up a new commission to investigate paper leaks. And the moment I get any inside information about that, rest assured, I'll bring you the breaking news!

In the Name of Development
Digging Deep!

Who isn't searching for God? Everyone is. But if you are, come to this town—Gaddapur! Here, your search will end, guaranteed, just like those ads promising cures for ringworm, eczema, piles, impotence, and even lost love.

Development and digging go hand in hand—like a bride and her veil. Wherever there's development, there's digging. Bridges, roads, buildings, towering structures—none of these can happen without excavation. The city's railway station is undergoing the 'Amrit Station' project, and as a result, it now looks like a battlefield of rubble and colossal craters—an epic tale of 'Amrit Kaal' unfolding in debris and dust.

The deeper the trenches of development, the deeper development seeps into our lives. And into these trenches, men and animals alike take unplanned dives. Especially during the monsoons, development refuses to stay confined to potholes and flows freely onto the roads. People drown in these "sacred waters" of development—some so profoundly that they attain ultimate salvation. Perhaps, this is what the scriptures referred to as "crossing the worldly ocean"!

The political foundations of our city are laid in these very potholes. Just take a look—digging everywhere! The whole city has become khudamayi—a land of perpetual excavation. Digging is no longer just an act here; it's a culture, a trademark! The municipality, the electricity department, the water department, and the citizens themselves are all devoted to preserving this legacy. If there's no digging in a particular area, people get an itch to start one.

Development in our city flows freely—like water! It passes right over people's heads—again, like water! The powers-that-be explain: "If we don't dig, development might escape elsewhere. We must trap it in potholes, lest rival regions hoard it for themselves." The city's drains, meanwhile, overflow with this water of progress during the rains, filling every street with the stench of advancement. Whether dogs, pigs, or humans—everyone revels in it!

Whether it's sewer lines or the so-called "Amrit Jal Pipeline," these open trenches welcome city dwellers with open arms. The ruling party hails them as the "lifelines" of the city. In fact, even parliamentary and assembly seats are won by riding on these very lifelines! Our town is so full of these "trenches of progress" that whenever one gets filled, people grow anxious. Without these holes, they suffer from indigestion—progress withdrawal symptoms!

Even common citizens do their part in sustaining this ecosystem. Be it for erecting a tent, installing a water pump, or laying a cable, fresh pits are dug with devotion. Progress piles up on roads in the form of debris, which is then carefully redistributed by the city's unpaid sanitation squad—cows, pigs, and dogs—who have been appointed without a tender. Since the paid, two-legged municipal staff is always on strike, these animals work

tirelessly to ensure progress reaches every doorstep—
"Development Delivered to Your Home!"

Shiny, smooth roads are an eyesore to the citizens; they cause them severe irritation. If people don't see development, they grieve as if they have lost a son! Whenever a new legislator takes office, the first order of business is to erase all traces of their predecessor's "development"—especially these sacred trenches! But the former legislator isn't one to back down either. After all, he had meticulously dug his progress holes all across the constituency, without any discrimination. Now, seeing his legacy being buried is unbearable!

Thus, he rallies the people and roars:

"Brothers and sisters, this new legislator is destroying our development! He's covering up our sacred potholes! This is a crime against the people! This is treachery! If we win the next election, we'll bring more progress! We'll dig new potholes— bigger, better, and deeper!"

And the crowd erupts in applause.

"Every inch of the road must become khudamayi! We'll bring in new schemes! Underground electric wires! Underground telephone cables! Underground gas pipelines! Soon, every speck of the city's road will be drenched in the divine spirit of digging!"

A thunderous applause shakes the air.

"Our leader must be like Khudi Ramji—forever digging, forever progressing!"

So You Must Be Happy!

"Hey, Dr. Sahab, how are you? You seem quite happy today. Looks like the rain has been good in the city!"

I was busy examining a patient in my OPD when my distant saala barged into my chamber. Now, whether a saala is near or distant, he remains a saala—entitled to disturb his jeeja whenever he pleases. Whatever little brain his sister has spared, he considers it his duty to chew on it constantly.

I had no choice but to pause my consultation. He was keenly observing my face, searching for some sign of happiness.

I replied, "Yes, of course, it's a reason to be happy. Rain benefits everyone! Farmers' faces light up, and they begin sowing. If the rain comes with hail, even the compensation departments light up with joy. Government offices always keep relief packages ready, just waiting for either floods or droughts—this in-between situation doesn't suit them.

If there's a flood, political parties will be 'concerned.' Newspapers will have headlines, TV debates will heat up, and news channels will get their much-needed TRP boost. Parties will get a golden opportunity to blame each other.

Rain also exposes the city's drainage system. Gutters overflow in celebration, potholes bloom in their full glory, and unsuspecting bikers and car drivers get drenched in mud, enjoying the 'splash' effect.

And households? Rainy days bring a special treat—husbands get an excuse to demand fried pakoras and tea. The cuckoos sing, self-proclaimed music enthusiasts mix Raag Malhar with Bollywood tunes, and monsoon frogs start their tar-tar orchestra.

Look at our city! We don't have a single water park, yet as soon as the monsoon arrives, the whole town turns into a massive water pool! People can swim, drown, or even enjoy water sports if they wish. Wooden planks outside shops serve as makeshift floaters. If the government wishes, they could stop draining this water and develop it into a natural water resource. Fish farming could become a booming industry. People could raise fish in front of their houses and enjoy fishing from their rooftops. And then? Government helicopters would drop food packets, and kids would practice their catching skills—perfect cricket training for the future.

Media houses thrive on such dramatic scenes. Headlines need catchy visuals. Writers, too, find new inspiration. The moment raindrops fall, their pens sharpen, and poetry flows. And, of course, poets from the Riti-Kaal tradition won't miss the chance to describe a rain-drenched damsel in all her youthful beauty."

I paused and looked at him. "But why do you think I'm happy?"

Without missing a beat, my saala grinned, "Come on, jeeja ji! You're an orthopedic doctor! Rainy season means booming business for you. People slip and fall, potholes on roads exist just for your benefit. The city's drainage ensures there's enough slush to keep the slips coming. Vegetable markets turn into obstacle courses. And let's not forget temple floors—polished marble, perfect for elderly devotees to have a divine fall and a direct meeting with God! Even godowns play their part in making sure people get injured. This season, jeeja ji, you must be making a fortune!"

I sighed. He had a point. Perhaps God sends rain solely to ensure orthopedic doctors have a steady income. Otherwise, who really needs it? And here I was, unnecessarily delivering a lecture to this 'enlightened' saala!

———

The Book Fair – A Grand Wedding Affair

A book fair is no less than a grand mass wedding ceremony. All around, books are decked up like brides, eagerly waiting for their veils to be lifted, while readers hover around like wedding guests—some genuinely looking for a literary match, others just there for snacks and the festive vibe.

The responsibility of bidding farewell to these bookish brides lies with the publishers, acting like father figures, persuading potential grooms (readers) to take them home. Every kind of book—desi, videsi, literary, mainstream—stands in a queue, awaiting their suitor's decision. The authors, meanwhile, have already performed their kanyadaan, handing over their manuscripts with a sigh of surrender.

At some stalls, authors are deeply engrossed in discussions, while elsewhere, curious wedding guests (readers) inspect the books with an air of importance. Then there are the professional vimochaks (book launchers), playing the role of the priests, solemnly chanting their launch mantras—sometimes inaugurating a book, sometimes indulging in a ceremonial muh dikhai (introducing the bride/book to society). Their half-hearted, pre-scripted book reviews sound just like the matrimonial classifieds—"Looking for a groom for a beautiful, cultured, and domestically skilled girl." Meanwhile, books from the rival camp are dismissed outright, with obituaries being sung in the deep, mournful tones of the Garuda Purana. All in all, this unique wedding procession is reveling in its own quirky splendor.

Back in the day, when I attended such fairs, I was more interested in the street food stalls than the books—just like in weddings, where the groom's family cares only about the rituals while the rest of the guests rush towards the buffet. At that time, books were merely an excuse to admire pustak-premikas (book-loving damsels)—some deeply engrossed in a book with a serious expression, others flipping through pages as if searching for a tragic love story. In those pre-selfie days, there was no way to capture oneself in pouts and weird angles, so one had no choice but to quietly admire the beauty of others.

Back then, "books" meant Surendra Mohan Pathak, Ved Prakash Sharma, Rakesh Kumar, and cheap, second-hand copies of Reader's Digest and Debonair! Reading literature was secondary—just owning old, yellowed books felt like possessing a vintage wine.

But now, the writing bug inside me has crawled out of its larva and pupa stages and fully evolved. So, attending the book fair this time was an entirely new experience. The crowd was still there, but there were noticeably more readers—especially Hindi readers. The younger generation seems to have taken a liking to books, but it's more of a trendy affair now—posing with books, posting selfies with hashtags like #WeLoveHindi, and declaring their literary romance online.

"Oh my God... This is Hindi... Hindi, I love you... Bole to..."— this is the new-age Bollywood-style love affair with Hindi!

There were more writers and book launchers than actual books. Some authors were desperately clinging to book launchers, while others were being dragged around by overenthusiastic publishers. The exchange of books was happening like the customary shagun ke notes (ceremonial cash gifts) at weddings:

- The first person hands over a [1] 100 note,

- The second person passes it to the third,

- The third to the fourth,

- And in the end, the same [1] 100 note lands back in the hands of the first person!

Just like that, authors were exchanging books amongst themselves—giving, taking, distributing. At some places, writers were being sold, at others, publishers were up for sale—but books? They seemed to be the least-sold item in this entire affair!

I even saw some publishers forcibly dragging authors to their stalls—exactly like vegetable vendors in Bhindi Bazaar! Their sales agents roamed around the aisles, latching onto wandering authors and leading them to their stalls.

"Sir, just have a look! Fresh arrivals… absolutely top quality! One glance, and you'll fall in love!"

At some stalls, due to acquaintances, I was loaded with books I may never open—but at least I can donate them to the city library!

If you plan to actually buy books, go prepared with a list. Otherwise, many Rambha-Urvashi type books will flirtatiously wink at you, tempting you with their seductive covers! Some stalls had transformed into full-fledged "book bars," where every book cover seemed to whisper:

"Come on, just one glance!"

Pro Tips for Surviving a Book Fair:

' Don't bring a tote bag—bring a trolley bag!

' Carry a water bottle!

' If possible, bring your own chair! (If you're not a celebrity author, no one will offer you a seat.)

' Keep a pen handy! (What if a charming reader asks for your autograph, and you end up borrowing a pen from them? Gayi bhains paani mein!)

Oh, and if you're a tea lover, be prepared to buy your own tea! Some authors had grandly declared on social media that chhole-bhature stalls would be conveniently located near publisher booths... but not even a single tea stall was found!

Being the penny-pincher that I am, I figured—why waste money on tea when I could buy a book for the same price? So, I had brought homemade parathas and pickle—my ultimate book fair survival kit!

I heard that Shashi Tharoor was having a session, but the path to the pavilion was so cunningly concealed that, after wandering in circles, I finally gave up. By then, my legs were more exhausted than my literary enthusiasm.

All in all, a great experience…

More than literature, I got to witness literary politics, trending authors, and the latest marketing gimmicks in action.

Next time, I'll go fully prepared—with a trolley bag, a chair, and a water bottle.

And yes, this time, I'll carry a damn good pen for autographs!

The Business of Charity
Neither Slow Nor Shady

Like every day, I was sitting in my chamber, figuring out ways to earn my daily bread. The relentless heat and rising temperature had already made it clear that this year, summer would arrive sooner than expected. I was entangled in my patients' never-ending queries when my phone rang.

Normally, I keep my phone on silent during OPD hours, but today, for some reason, it remained open for disturbances. Patients absolutely hate it when I take calls while listening to their ailments. If, mid-conversation, my phone rings, they glare at me as if a villain has just entered their romantic film scene. Panicked, I put my phone on silent.

It was an unknown number. I was sure it was either some bank eager to shove a loan down my throat, a company trying to sell me insurance for my already insured life, or a cyber fraudster attempting to fool me into some trap. I ignored the call and refocused on my patient, but soon, the phone screen lit up again. This time, instead of ringing, it vibrated fiercely in my pocket, making my whole body tremble.

The patient noticed this and, taking pity on me, said, "Doctor saab, pick it up!"

He said it with the same generosity as a boss granting an employee a two-day leave after relentless pleading.

Reluctantly, I picked up the phone.

"Guess who, Doctor Saab?" came a voice from the other end.

I racked my brain. The voice sounded like Gupta Ji, the head honcho of some charitable organization in town. But why was he calling from an unknown number? Then I realized—Gupta Ji probably knew that I rarely answered his calls. In fact, I had stored quite a few numbers in my phone just to remind myself not to answer them.

Cautiously, I asked, "Gupta Ji?"

"Ah! You recognized me. See, I'm outside your clinic with some people from our organization. We'd like to meet you. Just two minutes, and we'll be inside!"

Before I could utter a single word or cook up an excuse, the call was cut.

I felt trapped. I couldn't even lie and say I wasn't in the clinic— after all, the man had just called me from outside! I had no escape. It was clear—today, Gupta Ji had come to collect. My overzealous social service had finally caught up with me, and now, it was time to pay the dues—literally.

Gupta Ji's reputation for fundraising was legendary. One never knew when one's name might end up on his Most Wanted Donors list. My hands and feet trembled. Even an income tax raid would be less terrifying than a chanda vassooli (charity collection) raid. Half an hour passed.

They didn't come.

Twice, I peeked outside—still, no sign of them.

For a brief moment, I thought—could it be April 1st? Am I being pranked? But no, the dread remained. To calm my nerves, I attended to some more patients.

Just as I was about to step out for some air, a battalion of 8 to 10 men stormed in, led by none other than Gupta Ji.

From their familiar faces and the way some of them addressed each other as fufa ji (uncle-in-law) and jijaji (brother-in-law), it dawned on me—some were distant relatives. Not recognizing them was a grave crime on my part.

"Guess who?" one of them asked—the dreaded question that puts you in a fix.

Given my age and fading memory, I meekly admitted, "Sorry, I don't recall..."

"Doctor saab! We meet every morning during our walk!"

Oh! Right. Of course. I immediately put on my guilty-as-charged expression and apologized.

I tried to seat them in my OPD, hoping the patient rush would make them leave sooner. But they were one step ahead.

"No, no, Doctor Saab, let's sit upstairs in the drawing room. It's been a while since we had your wife's special tea!"

Trapped, I led them upstairs and quickly called my wife.

"Make tea for 10 people. Four without sugar. Hurry."

From the other end, I could hear her muttering:

"Who's here? How much are they asking for? Didn't they come last time too? These people do nothing but demand money! Don't get caught up in their nonsense!"

Anticipating this, I had already lowered the phone volume. I responded with standard, pacifying replies, "Yes, Gupta Ji and his team… Yes, tea for 10… Yes, make it quick… Maybe some snacks too… I'll send staff to help."

As soon as we sat down, one of the chanda warriors stretched his arm forward.

"Doctor saab, see this? My wrist still hurts. You treated it, but I had to go to Jaipur and spend [1] 10,000 more to finally get it fixed."

Ah! So this was a settlement case!

Before I could react, another member cut him off, "Doctor saab, we have a lot of complaints against you, but still, see? We came to you for a donation. That, itself, is an honor for you!"

Ah, the age-old donation = prestige trick! A classic!

Soon, one by one, the entire gang started reciting their well-rehearsed monologues.

One narrated the organization's timeline of great deeds—feeding the poor, helping children, supporting cows, and funding temples. My body hair stood on end. I was hearing such tales of nobility that even Florence Nightingale and Mother Teresa would take notes.

Another chimed in, "Doctor saab, your name is synonymous with generosity! You donate everywhere. We know. We have records."

Clearly, they had done their homework.

Finally, the grand moment arrived.

"Doctor saab, we won't take much. Just give what the others have given."

A receipt book was dramatically pulled out, as if it were a revolver about to seal my fate. The number on it was already filled in— far more than I had anticipated.

I swallowed hard. "This is too much. Have mercy. I'll give next year too, but right now, it's tax season—Income Tax is already after me!"

But the chanda mafia was unshaken. Their stance was as firm as a lawyer arguing his final case.

Gupta Ji's brows furrowed slightly. "Doctor saab, we don't ask just anyone. If it was about a small amount, I would've sent someone else. But we came personally. That should tell you how much respect we have for you."

Ah, reverse guilt-trip strategy! Masterful.

Cornered, I called my staff downstairs. There was no way I was asking my wife—I valued my life.

The staff brought the collection from the day's OPD earnings. Gupta Ji's team didn't even bother counting. "Who counts donations? We trust you, Doctor saab!" one said, snatching the bundle and triumphantly tearing off my receipt of surrender.

Mission accomplished.

As they exited, their victorious smirks said it all.

Downstairs, a patient at the reception was fuming, waving a [1] 500 note.

"What kind of clinic is this?! You don't keep change?"

Ah! Now I understood. I had just handed over all the change to The Business of Charity!

Back in my chamber, I saved another of Gupta Ji's unknown numbers in my phone—though I knew, next time, he'd call from yet another new number to keep this chanda vassooli dhanda running smoothly.

The Crowd and the Chaos

What do politicians really need? Just a bit of a crowd—who cares about the public otherwise? Speeches exist because of crowds, issues arise (or are raised) because of them. Politicians are nothing but humble bumblebees hovering over the flower of the crowd. Without a crowd, their wings lose all strength; the crowd is their flame, and they are its moths. On the battlefield of masses, they sow the seeds of promises with the plow of speeches and cultivate a crop of votes. If the crowd doesn't show up, they lock horns with the organizers.

And what don't they do to gather a crowd? These days, pulling in people is no easy feat! The public has become smart; these MGNREGA (rural employment scheme) folks have spoiled the game. All they care about is securing their daily wage. Whether they clap at a rally or toil in the fields—it makes no difference to them as long as they get their evening meal.

There's also a psychological aspect to crowds. From a psychological standpoint, for people like us, crowds are a sort of phobia, but for politicians, solitude is the real phobia—monophobia. The crowd is their intoxication, their fix. Without it, they go into withdrawal—sweating, palpitations, trembling hands and feet. Overcome by boundless anxieties, such politicians can often be heard asking, "What happened? Did the opposition lure away my crowd?"

In essence, the public is just a crowd. And this crowd behaves exactly like sheep penned in an enclosure. If kept together, they walk in unison—the proverbial sheep mentality. A leader's biggest USP is a crowd; it's their ticket to higher ranks in the party, their passage to Delhi, their claim to power, prestigious positions, commissions, and committees. The crowd even absolves scam-tainted leaders, helping them escape allegations. The crowd is both frenzied and blind—after all, vision gets obstructed in a mob.

The crowd is also crippled—it doesn't walk on its own. It follows a common vision, a universal direction—a direction that is manufactured, sponsored, and often handed out for free. And well, if something's free, even if it's poison, the crowd will accept it with open arms! The crowd doesn't have to go anywhere—it just has to stay put at one place.

The crowd is photogenic too. The strength of a leader is measured by the strength of their crowd at election rallies. In this country, unemployment, illiteracy, and poverty haven't flourished by accident; they serve a greater purpose—crowd generation! An educated person doesn't remain handicapped; their eyes open, and their mind starts breeding revolutionary ideas.

A crowd offers mass security—every lost, hopeless, and directionless individual feels safe in the herd. Even wolves don't hunt a lone sheep; they target flocks. A lone sheep can be fast, alert. But if one has to chase after each individual sheep, the task becomes arduous. Controlling a herd requires less effort, less time, and fewer resources.

If you look at a crowd from above, it appears exactly like a herd of sheep. And the moment a politician spots a crowd, the wolf within them awakens. They don't see people in the crowd; they see sheep waiting to be manipulated with their sharp claws. Their speeches flow effortlessly in front of a crowd—otherwise, their words remain stuck in their throats.

And here comes the leader, a good half an hour late. The organizers are drenched in sweat—the hall is nearly empty, save for a few committee members and their forcibly dragged-along family members. The event is about to begin, but the leader sits on stage, visibly bored.

Just nearby, a free food distribution (langar) was happening—devotees distributing offerings in the name of the Goddess. The crowd, which was supposed to be here, had diverted mid-way and flocked to the langar instead. The event was meant to be a lecture on 'Dimensions of Hindi Language Development', and a renowned Hindi scholar was invited as the guest speaker. He kept glancing at his watch, whispering to the organizers, "Shall we begin?"

The organizer, folding his hands, replied, "Sir, let it be. We'll schedule it some other time."

Despite much persuasion, the committee members refused to postpone the langar. But politicians always have a knack for turning situations to their advantage. Placing a reassuring hand on the organizer's shoulder, the leader smiled and said, "Let's go where our beloved public is. Let's partake in the Goddess's offerings as well."

And so, the entire team followed the leader to the langar. Because, after all, a crowd is everything—the leader knows it well. The crowd is the divine offering itself—the foundation of slogans, rallies, protests, lathi charges, spiritual discourses, bhajans, and religious rituals. The crowd is also statistics—record-breaking figures, headline-grabbing breaking news.

With a subtle nod, the leader signaled his PA—"Call the press. We have breaking news!"

"Leader XYZ, a devout follower of the Goddess, today graced Her devotees with his presence… for the first time in five years!"

The Epidemic of Disappearance

It seems like my city has caught an epidemic of disappearance. Every day, something or the other vanishes into thin air. People here are more distressed by what's missing than they are delighted by what they have. The city has become utterly self-centered. If politicians go missing, no one bats an eye. Roads disappear, bridges evaporate, relief funds vanish overnight, government schemes pull a Houdini act—one moment they exist, the next, poof! Rationed wheat, kerosene—gone, like a magician's trick. And yet, no one ever files a missing report. It's as if the entire city has been fed a dose of philosophical opium: What did we bring? What will we take? Whatever is here today might belong to someone else tomorrow. Whatever is lost today might reappear someday. Politicians make promises and then disappear, but the city knows they'll be back in five years, like clockwork. Office files disappear so frequently that people have stopped trusting them altogether. Files, after all, behave like stray thieves—always slipping away unless you leash them with a hefty bribe.

Now, it's not like the city doesn't compensate for these losses. When garbage bins disappeared, the municipality generously replaced them with potholes—perfect dumping spots for your trash. The drainage system lost its water, but don't worry—the streets are overflowing. If your bathroom shower isn't satisfying, just step outside—our roads have turned into public bathing ponds. The authorities also ensure that religious devotion remains intact. Stray animals roam the streets freely. Feel free to express your devotion—feed bread to stray dogs, chapatis to cows, or if you wish to dispose of your trash, just wrap it in plastic and serve it to the sacred cows. And for the sake of cattle lineage preservation, a few bulls have been released into the streets. These bulls, unfazed by societal decency, conduct genetic increment sessions in broad daylight—giving people a front-row seat to an uncensored, C-grade movie right in the middle of the road.

In fact, bullfights have become the city's prime source of entertainment. Why pay money to watch a bullfight in a stadium when you can witness one for free in the bustling streets? When two bulls lock horns and engage in a head-butting duel, even the shouting matches in parliament and TV news debates pale in comparison. Cockfights are a thing of the past—our municipal authorities have upgraded us to bullfights. There's action, thrill, collateral damage, and, of course, business for us orthopedic doctors.

The municipal council encourages us to stop mourning what's lost and instead celebrate what's still available. But for the past two years, something truly iconic has disappeared, something that defined our city's very soul. My dear Ganda Pur—oh, I mean Gangapur—was known for three things: juicy gossip, illegal gambling, and pigs. The first two still thrive, but the pigs—gone. Vanished. No one knows what wiped them out. Perhaps COVID took on a beastly avatar and eliminated them. The municipal council, of course, is patting itself on the back, calling it an achievement, but in reality, the city has lost an integral part of its identity. The golden era—or should I say, the pig era—is now merely a chapter in history, written in golden (or perhaps muddy) letters.

The iconic sights have changed. The roads, the filth, the puddles—all remain, but gone are the acrobatic pigs rolling joyfully in the muck. Let's be honest—these pigs were unofficial municipal employees, working tirelessly without wages. They handled sewage management, waste disposal, and early-morning human excretory clean-ups, all free of charge. They transported garbage from the streets to the drains. But now, they're all gone. It's like the city has been cursed—potholes and open drains eagerly wait for their return. Even the paigadaks (self-appointed street dwellers) find it lonely to roll in the filth without their beloved pig companions.

And let's not forget the silent traffic regulators—the pigs' extended family members, who once stood at intersections, waiting for a reckless driver to run over one of their own. If a piglet or an elder boar got run over, it was a day of celebration for the family—dinner was sorted! Special feasts were planned, and to top it off, the grieving family would extract a grieving fine from the driver—just like the traffic police, except without receipts.

Honestly, even the under-the-table income of traffic police officers took a hit with the disappearance of these pigs. The city now feels orphaned without them. To the esteemed city planners and development committees, I humbly request: Please take urgent action to compensate for this irreplaceable loss!

The Grass Chronicles

Today, my brain has truly gone out to graze. And look! The thought of writing about The Grass Chronicles has popped up too! Well, what can I do? My brain is like a buffalo—once it sits down to graze, it refuses to budge.

Grass—the one thing that should now be declared our National Herb. Its significance is so vast that for the common man, it is no less than Chyawanprash (the so-called elixir of life). Anyway, eating grass seems to be the only destiny left for humans, because the donkeys have long abandoned it in favor of Chyawanprash! Get the hint? And if I say anything more, you'll call me a blabbermouth!

Grass—it is fed, eaten, and spread. Grass is green, but these days, even its greenness is in question. Some people say the green color has started looking ideologically suspicious! So, a new breed of grass is being developed—yes, you heard it right— saffron-colored grass is on its way!

Meanwhile, in Netaji's backyard, I see some imported grass— never withers, always lush. But what about the grass that reached the common people? That, my friend, dried up into brittle twigs within days! The people protested:

"We were promised fresh, green grass! Why has it dried up?"

The government promptly responded:

"Grass wasn't just meant for eating; it was also meant for bedding... and for roofing!"

The people remained unconvinced. So, the government launched a new scheme—to ensure every citizen sees green grass, special glasses with green-tinted lenses were distributed. The moment people wore them—voilà! Everything turned lush green! Thunderous applause followed, celebrations broke out, and the government basked in its newfound glory.

Meanwhile, the grass in Netaji's garden had grown knee-high. He was pleased. He was told that walking barefoot on it absorbs the moisture of the grass, cooling the body. His loyal pawns, however, were already crawling through it like spineless earthworms, just waiting for Netaji's feet to grace them so they could feel blessed!

Grass is no longer just a local issue—it has become a crucial element of international diplomacy. Some nations literally survive on imported grass—all it takes is a begging bowl and a generous donor! Foreign policy now hinges on who is feeding whom and who is being ignored!

America, for instance, is a grass superpower. Nations line up, eyes pleading, waiting for America to throw some grass their way. If it obliges, diplomatic relations flourish; if not, all hell breaks loose!

Many countries knock on doors with desperate pleas:

"Brother, please throw us some grass! Our reputation is at stake!"

And what about our own country? Oh, we've imported foreign grass too—not to eat, but to show off!

"Look! We are being given grass too!"

The grass that is announced in manifestos is not meant to grow—it's merely a showpiece. In fact, sometimes, the country's own grass is secretly uprooted and deposited in foreign banks, safe from our tax system's prying eyes. There, it flourishes, waiting to return as NRI Grass!

The common man only asks for a little grass. But even for that, politicians come running, dangling promises like green fodder before a cow. And the people? Oh, they chew on it happily. Election season is like monsoon for them—a blind man in monsoon sees only greenery! Once elections are over, they continue to see lush landscapes in their dreams for the next five years.

For the common man, whether it's grass or kerosene, it hardly makes a difference anymore!

For politicians, however, grass has become a precious commodity. So precious that opposition leaders are being lured into switching sides with the promise of exclusive, organic grass! Corruption scandals are now breaking out over grass supplies!

The elite's backyards are lush, while bureaucrats chew on bribe-flavored grass, happily ruminating.

"The Grass Chronicles" simply echoes what the Bible once said:

"All flesh is grass."

Or in simpler terms—"Grass is life, and life is grass!"

The Marketplace of Curses

A Satirical Take on the Modern Swearing Culture

There was a time when songs like "Ladki Kamaal Dekho, Ankhiyon Se Goli Maare…" (Look at this marvelous girl, shooting bullets from her eyes) ruled the charts. Ah, what an era! But times have changed, and bullets seem to have become too expensive. Neither can they wound anymore, nor can the piercing gaze of a lover strike deep. And so, a new age has dawned—the era of curses!

We now have a self-automated curse production line in full swing. Just add a pinch of shamelessness, a dash of audacity, and a generous helping of brazenness to your system, and voilà! Curses will start rolling out naturally.

Our country spends billions on ammunition, pouring trillions into defense budgets. Some nations dedicate a significant chunk of their GDP to weaponry. So, why not mass-produce curses and turn them into an export commodity?

Let's welcome our enemies—not with bullets, but with a barrage of expletives!

In fact, we should establish a dedicated research wing to study the art of swearing. When it comes to profanity, our country is truly self-reliant—100% Made in India! We need to dig deep into the history of curses. Whether or not you take pride in your nation's past, whether or not you wish to rewrite history, one thing is certain—if we document the history of cursing, we might just restore our lost national glory.

Curses are the great equalizer. They transcend class, caste, and wealth. No money is exchanged—just a simple trade of one curse for another, preferably with a 25% bonus insult in return!

We should even have a Code of Conduct for this:

Curses must be repaid with curses—nothing more, nothing less.

Any retaliation involving slaps, punches, or kicks should be deemed a criminal offense.

Cursing should be a mandatory subject in school curriculums. Imagine a nation where every street, every alley, every corner resounds with the symphony of swearing!

Curses—the ultimate qualification for political party spokespersons.

Curses—the lead actors in never-ending debates on news channels.

Curses—equal-opportunity offenders, sparing no one—from mothers to brothers, from friends to foes.

In fact, let's tap into our unemployed, reel-addicted youth and engage them in the creative expansion of profanity. This would not only generate employment but also unleash their natural talent to its fullest potential.

Frankly, I propose that our elite swearers be deployed to the borders. A couple of well-timed verbal assaults could take down a handful of terrorists!

After all, markets run on demand and supply—and curses? They were once the very heartbeat of our regional culture—woven into daily life, festivals, traditions, and even the rituals of birth and death.

Cursing isn't just about anger or frustration—it's an expression of love, affection, mockery, disgust, and even endearment. The tragedy is that once curses were hijacked by the 'Page Three' elite, no one bothered to consult their original creators! This is a blatant violation of copyright laws, and we ought to file a lawsuit.

The market has completely rebranded curses. Once a proud feature of rural dialects, they are now reserved for celebrities, YouTube influencers, and high-society urbanites. The act of cursing has shifted from being something spoken to something performed.

Cursing has become a spectacle. Once an integral part of folk culture, it has now been commercialized and mismanaged beyond recognition.

OTT platforms, social media reels, reality shows—everywhere, curses are being served with a side of nudity, vulgarity, and obscenity. The situation has become so dire that even curses themselves are feeling ashamed!

For heaven's sake, at least do some research before you start swearing! The intonation, facial expressions, and emotional depth of a curse matter! Come visit our rural heartlands, and we'll teach you the true art of swearing.

Even women curse, but with their faces veiled. Even in profanity, there's an elegance, a distinct tone, a style!

Take the word "saale." To you, it might simply mean "brother-in-law," but in our linguistic arsenal, it is a hot-selling product— a versatile swear word that can express affection, insult, anger, love, frustration, or contempt depending on the intonation, facial gestures, and vocal frequency!

In essence, our true mother tongue is profanity! Whatever little standard words you manage to grasp in between are nothing but punctuation marks—mere commas and full stops in the grand narrative of expletives!

All we await now is for the government to declare cursing the official national language. Hopefully, by the next election, the ruling party will at least include it in the list of recognized languages.

You city-bred elites will never truly understand the real flavor of swearing!

The Politics of Fun:
The Joyful Philosophy of Indian Life

The world of the common Indian is a vibrant, high-spirited carnival where every activity must have a pinch of fun and frolic. Though global Happiness Index reports may rank us behind other countries, that's just a statistical illusion. The rigid parameters of the World Happiness Index fail to grasp the innate masti (carefree enjoyment) and entertainment ingrained in every Indian's DNA. Here, people firmly believe that any task devoid of joy is pointless. Enjoyment isn't confined to action alone—it must be seen, heard, and felt. After all, as they say, "Life is a punishment if there's no fun in it." Even among the four purusharthas—dharma (duty), artha (wealth), kama (desire), and moksha (liberation)—fun must be seamlessly woven in.

Where there's fun, there's an instant "Wah Bhai Wah!" (Bravo!), and where it's missing, there's only one response—"Bhai, maza nahi aaya!" (Brother, it wasn't fun!). Political parties have now mastered this art and are stuffing their election manifestos with promises of fun, served hot and spicy to the public. The gullible electorate, enchanted by this promise of endless amusement, is blissfully waiting for the arrival of acche din (better days). And just to ensure the audience engagement, politicians in their rallies frequently ask, "Bhai, maza aaya ki nahi?" (Brother, did you have fun or not?).

Now, you can slap a foreign label on it—call it "kick," "twist," or "thrill"—but in Indian life, it remains our good old maza in its raw, unfiltered form. You can rob the common man in broad daylight, but as long as you give him some entertainment, he won't even complain. Real development metrics may fill government reports, but they can never satisfy the public's appetite for fun! If our lackluster democracy still has a heartbeat, it's only because of this elixir of maza, which is generously poured down our throats by politicians, bureaucrats, journalists, and artists alike. As for democracy? Chalta rahega! (It will keep going). After all, we have a golden saying—"Feed buffaloes fodder and governments statistics"—this is the essence of real democracy!

The Four Pillars of Entertainment Democracy

The four pillars of democracy—judiciary, executive, legislature, and media—have now recognized the national pulse and are devoted to ensuring that the public is thoroughly entertained. Because, let's be honest, entertainment without engagement is no entertainment at all! This fact is well understood by our news channels, spiritual leaders, educators, artists, and politicians. The national mantra now echoes in unison—"Entertainment, entertainment, and entertainment!"

But the real flag-bearers of this movement are our journalists. Whether it's TV news, print media, or digital platforms, their primary mission is no longer informing the public—it is entertaining them. News is now seasoned, spiced, and served with extra masala (sensationalism). TV channels have taken it up a notch by organizing qawwali-style debate shows, stand-up comedy-styled news reports, and, of course, the iconic TV panel debates, where only the loudest and most aggressive panelists are invited. What are these debates, if not a mega theatrical drama—a puppet show with scripted outrage? The bigger the spectacle, the bigger the TRP!

When there's no news, don't worry, news will be created. No incidents happening? No problem! First, the breaking news is aired, then the event is staged to match it. Media trials are now being conducted live; crimes are solved and verdicts are delivered—all within a 30-minute debate slot. Watching these debates reminds one of the bygone nawabi (royal) era, when aristocrats entertained themselves by making roosters fight. Every expletive, every slur, every insult hurled is pre-scripted, rehearsed, and timed for maximum impact. Even the anchors take a few blows to appear neutral and avoid being labeled as godi media (lapdog media).

On these shows, the more a panelist abuses and shouts, the higher their ranking. No wonder, we now have a rising star—"Gaali Wali Madam" (The Lady of Expletives), who has mastered the art of verbal assault. In fact, these spokespersons should be given National Film Awards for Best Supporting Actor in a Political Drama! Because at the end of the day, who needs logical discussions when you can have T20-style verbal duels?

Fun-Infused Spirituality & Education

Our spiritual leaders and politicians have also adapted to the entertainment economy. Sermons and speeches are now customized with spicy dialogues, dramatic pauses, and theatrical gestures. Religious discourse is no longer about jnana (wisdom)—it is about tamasha (spectacle).

This obsession isn't limited to politics and media; even education has been swept into this maza-maya (illusion of fun). Depth of knowledge? Irrelevant. What matters is how engagingly a teacher can present it. Students prefer the classroom where the professor cracks jokes, mimics characters, and turns lectures into stand-up comedy gigs. Without maza, knowledge itself becomes boring and thus useless!

Social Media: The Ultimate Maza Bazaar

Nowhere is this culture of maza more visible than on social media. Here, virality is directly proportional to the entertainment quotient of a post. A tweet with humor gets a million shares, while a serious, well-researched post gets lost in oblivion. The fun economy is booming—memes, reels, and jokes now define our collective consciousness.

In earlier times, maza was a behind-the-closed-doors indulgence. Now, it's a full-blown open-market commodity. Gone are the days when jesters entertained kings in private courts. Today, they do it for likes, shares, and monetized views.

Even Spirituality is Marketed with Maza

The common Indian, forever in pursuit of maza, now finds it even in religious discourses. Whether in spiritual congregations, motivational seminars, or daily office gossip—entertainment is the binding force. Gone are the days when sages sat in solitude for enlightenment. Today's spiritual leaders must perform like rockstars, complete with dramatic pauses, stage lighting, and background music.

And why not? With devotional songs now remixed into Bollywood-style beats, why should spiritual discourses remain dull? Mega satsangs (spiritual congregations) are now full-fledged concerts, complete with DJs, LED screens, and celebrity performances. Ram naam ki loot hai, loot sako toh loot lo! (The divine name of Ram is up for grabs—grab as much as you can!) The marketization of faith has reached new heights. From designer mala beads to luxury yoga retreats, religion is now a blockbuster industry. Even the saints themselves double as models in their own product commercials—because what better way to promote pure desi maza than through its own brand ambassadors?

Final Thought: Welcome to the Republic of Maza!

At the end of the day, the Indian common man—be it at work, at prayer, or in his daily struggles—remains a devoted disciple of maza. Whether through a flirtatious glance from a neighbor, a swig of liquor after a long day, or watching a street fight for free entertainment—fun is always just around the corner. Our spiritual leaders and motivational speakers know this well—without stage performance, their impact is negligible. Today, a preacher must be a stand-up comedian, a teacher must be an entertainer, and a politician must be a reality show contestant.

In this grand bazaar of maza, where democracy itself thrives on entertainment, one thing is certain—India may not top the Happiness Index, but it surely remains the undisputed superpower of fun!

"Maza-e-Hindustan, Zindabad! "

Budget: A Bitter Pill or a Sweet Treat?

I was just strolling down the road when I bumped into Budget. He had dark sunglasses on and a scarf wrapped around his face— just like how girls zoom past these days without a care in the world. He was trying to slip away, knowing very well that I have a habit of poking my nose into things. But I blocked his way.

"Hey, Budget Bhai, why the cold shoulder? Where are you sneaking off to like this?"

"Oh no, you recognized me!"

"Of course, I did! You're all over the newspapers and TV these days. But tell me, Budget Bhai, you're known as the budget of the common man, yet you won't even make eye contact with him. Why so?"

Budget smirked, "Brother, forget me for a second—can you even manage your own household budget? Look, I may belong to the common man, but I'm no longer just a 'common budget.' I've been given a VIP makeover! It's not just my color that has changed—my quality, my distribution, my entire foundation has been restructured. I am now categorized based on color, religion, and caste. The moment I take birth in the Parliament's delivery room, ministers, bureaucrats, and tycoons queue up to adopt me. And you, the common man, who spends his day juggling between flour, lentils, and salt, how do you plan on handling me?"

Throwing in his final justification, Budget continued, "Look, I'm like those government buildings whose construction is announced every year. The poor, living in slums, are shown the dream that they'll get a house in it. The middle class strengthens the foundation with their tax money, but in the end, the allocation always goes to the powerful. A few well-connected folks do manage to sneak in with some 'setting' and 'approach.' The corporate houses are handed over the maintenance contract, while the security of the building is given to government officers. But the ownership? That always remains in the hands of those in power. And if a coalition government is in place, then even the ownership gets a 'joint registration.'

"As for the opposition, their only job is to find flaws in the building's design, construction material, and structure. But let's be honest, even they don't want the slum dwellers, for whom the building was promised, to actually start living there. Because if they do, then where will the 'election rhetoric' come from? The opposition needs them in slums—to cry over their miseries, to highlight their suffering. After all, how else will they craft their electoral lamentations?"

I asked, "Budget Bhai, but surely, there must be something in it for the common man?"

"Of course, there is! There are concerns, commissions, committees, endless surveys, and statistics. But the common man just doesn't understand! He clings to his poverty like a politician clings to his chair! The poor are stubborn—they know that as long as they remain poor, they'll remain a priority. Their plight keeps politicians and officials busy round the clock. News channels dedicate their prime-time slots to discussing poverty. Intellectuals spend their wisdom delivering long lectures on it."

I probed further, "But what about the unemployed? Shouldn't there be something for them?"

Budget coughed, struggling to swallow my troublesome question, and then responded, "Of course! I take special care of the unemployed. Haven't you noticed? Mobile data, WiFi, and the internet have all been made dirt cheap. Now, the unemployed can create reels all day long, stay glued to online surfing, and convince themselves that unemployment is just a myth! It's all in the mind.

"And you know, poverty is a 'relative term.' Take Mr. Sharma from next door—he considers himself poor because his Maruti 800 looks like a toy car next to your brand-new Creta. Seth Dhansukh Lal became 'poor' the moment GST was implemented. Many builders turned 'poor' after demonetization. And remember that raid on Lala Bitukdas? He had to endure several days of poverty—until the high command stepped in to 'resolve' the issue."

"Look, as long as I exist, debates exist! As long as I exist, there's chaos in Parliament! Without me, politics would be like a classic movie—no drama, no action, no comedy! I am the secret spice that makes the political stew flavorful.

"Thanks to me, economists and intellectuals get to weave magical figures and present them as artistic masterpieces—just like abstract art, which no common man can understand! When the common man looks at these twisted statistics, he feels like he's stepped into a mystical world. And he finds solace in the fact that at least his name is attached to something grand—'The Common Man's Budget!'

"They always name me after the common man, but the reality is, I exist only to fill the pockets of the elite."

By now, Budget, who had been a little hesitant earlier, had completely let loose. "And you! You never leave me alone! The moment I arrive in the market, you start writing all sorts of nonsense about me. Look, I am the nation's budget! First, worry about your own household budget. Hasn't your home minister given you [1] 100 to buy vegetables? And yet, you siphoned off [1] 20 for cigarettes! If you don't behave, I'll complain to your home minister!"

And with that, Budget bolted, leaving me standing there, speechless.

The Tragic Tale of a Desire

For the past ten days, I have been lying abandoned in the minister's office, buried in a corner of the trash bin. On top of me are countless helpless sisters like me—hapless recommendation letters, invitations, greetings, and petitions— all piling up, crushing me under their weight. It has become hard to breathe. The garbage collector hasn't come for two days.

My last wish is to at least escape this suffocation and reach a recycling plant, where I might serve some purpose for the nation.

It would have been better if I had been thrown onto the streets. Perhaps a scrap dealer would have sold me as waste paper. At least I could have found a purpose—serving as a plate for some street vendor's samosas or becoming a paper boat for a child, sailing briefly through the potholes filled with rainwater.

But no! You, the so-called human, with your petty recommendation, walked into the minister's office empty-handed, as if you were bestowing a royal decree. Do you have any sense at all? When you had the MLA write me, he had clearly told you, "Brother, I have no power in this matter." Yet, he still wrote it—because you insisted. Fool! He was indirectly telling you that he had no real authority. Until you put something into his hands, what did you expect from a mere desire written on paper?

I knew my fate the moment you brought me here, carrying me like some grand proclamation from the Red Fort. My master, the one who had me written, cannot even get his own son's work done without greasing palms. And you? You are nothing but an insignificant voter.

Your memory is short. In five years, you'll forget everything, just like a typical voter. Right now, the MLA still cares for your family because your household holds a hundred votes. Otherwise, you wouldn't even be allowed near his bungalow gate. Didn't you see what he did to win your vote? He called someone your uncle, someone else your brother-in-law, another your father, and another your grandfather. And your grandfather? Oh, he left no stone unturned—digging up past grievances, making the MLA grovel. But the MLA came prepared—his nose isn't made of flesh but solid steel; it won't wear down.

Now your time is up—finished! Now it's the MLA's time to rule, fool!

I have seen how desires arrive here in grand style, wrapped in glittering envelopes, their bulging bellies making it clear how "weighty" they are. Watch how the MLA kisses them, handing them over to his secretary. The secretary carefully marks them, neatly filing them away. And me? Do you remember what happened to me? The minister flung me away as if he had found a venomous snake—afraid I might bite him!

But no, you had to be a righteous idiot! Your obsession with not giving bribes has driven the MLA up the wall. You've harassed so many people—calling the councillor, the block officer— forcing them to lie just to avoid you. The chairman had to pretend he was in Delhi one day and Jaipur the next just to get rid of you. You don't even realize how the same lowly party worker you once mocked as a sanitation worker has now become the MLA's personal assistant.

Don't you get it? The moment you got me written, the minister's office received a call telling them to ignore me. Even if you spent seven generations trying to decipher the MLA's cunning smile, you wouldn't succeed. You keep making calls—sometimes through the chairman, sometimes through the MLA's old school teacher, sometimes through some distant relative who, ironically, the MLA absolutely despises! For ten days, you've been camping at the MLA's house, stuffing yourself with tea and snacks. The MLA has blocked your number, yet you refuse to take the hint.

And now, look at your precious 'Desire'—tossed into the trash, buried under garbage. Are you satisfied? First, you annoyed the MLA. Now, for ten days, the minister's office has been making a fool out of you—telling you, "Sir is in the bathroom." And you? You still won't back off.

Now, tell me—should the minister not even take a dump in peace? Should he not bathe? If he spends ten hours in the bathroom, why should it bother you? Are you a minister? No! You're not even a peon! You have no idea that all important government business—negotiations with high command, strategies to frame opponents, deals with local goons, planning scams—are all discussed in the bathroom! It is the only place left untouched by sting operations.

So now, the minister is busy scrubbing his sins clean—washing his hands, blackened by corruption, and his kurta, stained with the blood of the poor. And you? You, my dear owner, are nothing but a fool in this grand democratic circus—a mere voter, with no value beyond a single ballot.

Victims of Misunderstanding

In today's world, feeding oneself is no easy task, but feeding misunderstandings? Oh, that's effortless! The best part? It doesn't even cost a dime. Misunderstandings grow on their own—you won't even realize when they've matured from infancy to adulthood, from naïve to full-blown troublemakers.

Take neighborhood girls, for example. Parents might be the last to know when their daughters hit adulthood, but the nosy neighbors? They've been keeping track from day one. The local loafers sense a girl's coming-of-age long before Sharma Ji's family even starts planning her wedding. That's society for you—whether it's a growing girl or a growing misunderstanding, both spark heated discussions in the alleys before reaching their own homes. No one notices their own daughter growing up, but the moment someone else's does, the world turns into an expert panel.

Be it politics, domestic life, or professional spheres—misunderstandings are the foundational bricks in the grand structure of deception. They are weak, helpless creatures, always looking for a nurturing hand to feed them, to raise them with care. And let's be honest, they're charming—so charming that you'd feel like cradling them, rocking them to sleep in your arms.

But beware! Misunderstandings don't just exist to be victims; they are predators too. The kind of predator that—how do I put it—'kills the snake without breaking the stick.' Your boss might prey on you with one, your backstabbing friend might use one against you, or a so-called well-wisher might be silently sharpening one to bring you down.

The new-age political hopefuls in town are all victims of misunderstanding. 'This time, the party ticket is definitely mine!' They stake their homes, families, businesses—everything on this belief. But politics, my friend, is an ecosystem sustained by misunderstandings. If you don't keep feeding them, nothing moves.

I, too, have been a victim of misunderstandings. At one point, I believed I could become a great singer; at another, I thought I'd launch a startup and become the next Tata or Birla. But the moment my misunderstanding grew big enough, I buried it deep in my chest. I never let it reach adulthood.

The world itself runs on misunderstandings. They are like the engine oil that keeps life's machinery running smoothly. The problem arises when people mistake them for the fuel. That's when they hit a dead end. Some people survive solely on the oxygen of misunderstandings—take that away, and life would become unbearable.

Take the human condition—people live under the grand misunderstanding that they will never die. This is why they keep preparing for seven generations ahead. How many monuments, tombs, and memorials stand today as testaments to this grand illusion? Pigeons, for instance, are under the misunderstanding that these monuments were built for their excretion. The stray dogs think they exist as makeshift lampposts for their raised legs. But man? He foolishly assumes that he is here for eternity and keeps hoarding pickles for the years ahead.

I remember my grandfather once meticulously preparing jars of pickles during the summer, planning to savor them in winter. After all, aged pickles taste the best, right? But before winter arrived, so did his final departure. He never got to taste his prized pickles.

Misunderstandings are either adopted or imposed; no one is born with them. Many parents fail to raise their children properly, but they excel at raising the misunderstanding that their child will one day make them proud.

That said, misunderstandings aren't entirely bad. They are the driving force behind legendary love stories—Laila-Majnu, Heer-Ranjha, and countless others. Lovers promise to pluck stars from the sky under the spell of a beautiful misunderstanding. Without it, no romance would ever take off.

I have a friend who has a passion for nurturing misunderstandings, willing to go to any lengths for them. We once shared a mutual misunderstanding—that we were inseparable companions in each other's joys and sorrows. Turns out, his misunderstanding has long since faded; mine still lingers.

We once joined an organization together. The moment we stepped in, he nurtured a misunderstanding that the entire weight of the institution rested on his shoulders. Soon, his shoulders began to slump. He became so troubled that he frequently threatened to resign. The rest of the members, equally troubled by his delusion, nurtured a new misunderstanding of their own—that the organization could function perfectly fine without him.

The two misunderstandings clashed. My friend's illusion came crashing down. Misunderstanding bid him farewell, whispering, 'I'm leaving for now, but when you join another organization, I'll come running back to you. I belong to you—I simply can't live without you!'

Marriages are built on the misunderstanding that one will find a beautiful, well-mannered, domestically skilled wife. Politics thrives on a stale pudding of misunderstandings, served with a sweet glaze of promises, slogans, and grand schemes. The public keeps these misunderstandings alive, while politicians fatten themselves in their comforting shade.

Misunderstandings aren't necessarily wrong. If a husband doesn't harbor the illusion that 'a man who loves his wife can't possibly refuse household chores,' then tell me—who will do the dishes, the laundry, and the cooking? This 'Best Husband' misunderstanding alone is keeping countless households from falling apart.

Back in college, many hostel mates fell victim to misunderstandings daily. A girl borrowing a practical notebook, glancing back, or simply asking someone's name—this was all it took for them to adopt a baby misunderstanding. 'She's your future wife,' they'd declare, performing an imaginary baby shower for the newborn illusion.

Within a day, these misunderstandings would go through an entire cycle—wedding, reception, honeymoon, and even baby names. But by the next morning, the illusion would wander into the girls' hostel, only to return with a wounded heart, lamenting, 'I came to hunt, but got hunted instead.'

Misunderstandings happen. Once, I submitted a satirical piece to a publisher. To my surprise, they printed it in the newspaper the very next day! No rejections, no delays—just immediate publication. Overwhelmed, I typed out a heartfelt thank-you message to the editor. The response I received? 'Dr. Sahab, we'll keep publishing your articles… just make sure we get a big hospital advertisement on Janmashtami.'

I watched in real time as my grand misunderstanding collapsed like a sandcastle against the tide. But honestly, whether good times come or not, is there really any harm in nurturing a few good misunderstandings along the way?

Borrowed Newspaper

I had just returned from my morning walk, having shed half a kilo in sweat, when my eyes landed on an abandoned newspaper. Usually, newspapers don't lie around like orphans. My neighbor, Mr. Sharma, snatches mine from the hawker before it can even touch the ground. He reads it first, lets his dog read whatever remains, and then hands me the tattered, pitiable remnants. Of course, he never forgets to add his expert commentary:

"Dr. Garg, who even subscribes to newspapers these days? That too this newspaper? Haven't you heard? XYZ newspaper is all the rage now! This one's useless—filled with government tenders, wedding classifieds, and third-page gossip about film stars."

Mr. Sharma discontinued this "useless" newspaper long ago. He has his reasons—some real, some purely fictional. The real reason is that he took four years (and countless arguments) to pay off a six-month newspaper bill. The fictional ones include: "My wife's sleep gets disturbed by the hawker's cycle bell in the morning." And his all-time favorite:

"I gave up on this third-class newspaper ages ago! But I still read it—for your sake—so that you don't have to suffer through it."

Many times, I have felt the urge to say, "Sharma ji, if that's the case, why not just subscribe to another paper?" But the sheer weight of his generosity—his sacrifice of reading my so-called worthless newspaper—keeps me silent.

It's not like I haven't tried to discontinue it. Once, I even switched to another newspaper. But the hawker, in his infinite wisdom, decided to deliver both. Frustrated, I called the newspaper agency. Their response?

"Oh, Dr. Sahab, why are you being so petty? The newspaper isn't just for you, is it? Shouldn't there be a few newspapers in your hospital's waiting hall? Patients and medical reps need something to read too! And if you don't cooperate with us, how can we cooperate with you? You know, we get so many complaints about your hospital… but we make sure they don't get published."

This subtle threat was enough to shut me up. So, I quietly went back to my old newspaper.

But today, I was surprised to find it lying orphaned on my doorstep. Turns out, Mr. Sharma was visiting his in-laws. I picked it up half-heartedly, and out fell a pamphlet.

Newspapers these days come with an avalanche of pamphlets—bright, glossy, and in all sizes, nestled inside like a mother dog nursing ten puppies. Perhaps this trend began during the Emergency when underground activists would distribute anti-government leaflets.

Pamphlets are now flooding the city. The moment you pick up a newspaper, two or three pamphlets drop out—school admissions, visiting doctors from out of town, astrologers promising miracles, ointments for rashes and mysterious diseases, coaching classes, or some newly opened showroom.

Advertisements that once graced our walls now arrive at our doorstep in newspapers. Those guaranteed cures for secret diseases—which once adorned public toilet walls—now reach every home. No wonder public toilet footfall has decreased!

Poor newspapers have become beasts of burden—once tasked with carrying half-baked news, now also loaded with pamphlets.

For days, I have been deprived of the joy of picking up my newspaper—thanks to my dear neighbor. On my way back from my morning walk, I only find pamphlets strewn on the ground, while Sharma ji walks off with my newspaper. He knows I am not particularly interested in reading it anyway. So, he reads it for me, filters out the "important" news, and delivers it to me in digest form—over a cup of sweet tea at my place.
You see, at home, Sharma ji's wife has banned sugar.
Thus, a routine has developed. Every morning, as soon as the newspaper arrives, Sharma ji pounces on it. He sets up his chair in the courtyard while his wife hands him a cup of sugarless tea. He then devours the entire newspaper—twice. Nothing is left unread—not even obituaries, wedding announcements, or condolence messages. When he's done, he solves the crossword and marks important articles by artistically doodling over them. If something truly catches his eye, he clips it out for his personal archive.

Even after all this, if he still isn't satisfied, he passes the paper to his dog—who, blessed by nature with both a keen nose and a literary bent, reads it the only way he knows how: by chewing and digesting it.

By the time the remains of the newspaper reach me, they resemble the pothole-ridden roads of our city—full of holes where articles used to be.

Once, I was out of town for a month. But Sharma ji, ever so considerate, ensured I did not miss my newspaper. He simply took it home with him.

A month later, when I returned, the hawker arrived with the bill. It struck me that a month's worth of newspapers must have piled up at Sharma ji's place. So, I thought—why not collect them? My wife, after all, regularly calls the scrap dealer at the end of the month. Perhaps this is her small contribution to the Swachh Bharat Abhiyan.

I asked Sharma ji for the month-old newspapers.

My request did not sit well with him. With a look of mild disgust, he said:

"Oh, Dr. Garg, you should have told me earlier! That pile had become a menace! My dog kept pulling newspapers out and scattering them all over the house. Just yesterday, I sold the whole lot to the scrap dealer."

As I walked back home, I realized that Sharma ji had done one more favor for me. He had lightened my burden—by ensuring I didn't have to deal with the waste of old newspapers!

Big Talk from Big People, Ji!

He's a *very* big man, you see. But even bigger than the man himself are his "big talks" — grand statements that echo through every alley and neighborhood, always perched on people's tongues.

Honestly, who hasn't dreamt of becoming a "big man" one day? I had that dream too. In fact, from childhood itself—not to grow up quickly per se, but to become *someone important* was a burning desire. Kids today, though, aren't obsessed with becoming *big men*—they just want to grow up fast. Sometimes even more so, their parents do.

Back then, I would constantly scan my surroundings, trying to figure out who the real *big man* was. At one point, the school peon who rang the bell seemed like the ultimate big shot to me. I mean, think about it—he controlled when school began and when it ended! We didn't understand the concept of *len-den* (give-and-take) at that age. If we had, maybe we'd have bribed him to ring the dismissal bell early! But that illusion shattered the day I saw him begging our headmaster for two days' leave.

Then the headmaster became our new model of a *big man.* I began dreaming of becoming like him. The moment he entered school, the entire place would freeze as if someone had been *saanp soongh gaya ho* (bitten by silence). Every morning, he'd make a couple of students *murga* (a punishment pose) and whip a few others with a thin stick—as if that was his breakfast. Then he'd retreat to his chamber and spend the rest of the day barking orders at teachers. I thought—now *that's* the kind of authority and aura I want! But even that dream crumbled when a government inspector visited, and I saw our same fearsome headmaster groveling before him.

And so went the cycle—we dreamt of being magicians, halwais (sweet-makers), singers, actors, dancers… anything and everything. Somehow, becoming a doctor never crossed our minds as a "big" ambition—maybe because doctors gave injections, and we hated both giving and receiving those!

Though yes, becoming a policeman did sound exciting. The mere mention of *police* sent tremors through the whole village! I once expressed this desire to my parents. But instead of encouragement, they warned me that if the police ever got wind of someone wanting to become like them, they'd arrest him on the spot!

As we grew up, so did our disillusionment. One thing became clear—there's a vast difference between an "object" and a "big man." See something from afar, and it looks small; get closer, and it appears in its real size. But with big men, it's the opposite. From a distance, they look larger than life. But up close? Sometimes so small, so petty, that you feel disgusted.

Being a big man works a lot like the theory of relativity. You're only as big as long as there's no one bigger standing next to you. The moment someone more powerful shows up, *your* big man begins to shrink—especially through his behavior. His grand stature starts to unravel, and he appears exposed. The proud, upright back slouches, and suddenly, he's crawling. The world is full of these illusions. People are jostling and elbowing each other to *become* big men. And once they do, they repay those old bruises with interest—by shoving the ones below them.

They've become *big people*, yes. But whether true greatness lies underneath the surface? That's another matter altogether. In fact, the bai (maid), the peon, the servant in such elite homes often whisper the most biting truths about these "big men's" fragile humanity and hollow sensitivity.

Still, big people are big, sir. And their *big talk* is even bigger. As long as they're alive, even if their *dog* dies, the whole town turns up for the *terahveen* (13th-day mourning ceremony). But the day *they* die? If even four people show up to carry their corpse on the bier, you'd consider it a blessing.

In the end, the illusion that truly shattered was this: a *big man* is not the one who appears grand while living, but the one whose goodness and dignity people still remember after he's gone.

Anyway, what do I know? I'm just a small man, after all. Why get into arguments with the big folks? Let them keep having their *bade-bade baatein*—Big Talk from Big People, Ji!

Just Two Words

They say one should use words wisely. Words are those weapons that can wound, and also heal. They are considered divine in form—*brahm-svaroopa*. Perhaps that's why the concept of *do shabd* (two words) was born. On public platforms, it is often seen that a speaker is invited to say *do shabd*. But the truth of *do shabd* goes much deeper than that.

Words should be spent sparingly, which is why silence is called the ornament of fools. Because if a fool remains silent, it's tolerable, but the moment they speak, their foolishness becomes evident. Sometimes I feel that even those draped in the cloak of so-called wisdom are asked to say *do shabd* only to expose them. I've often seen that when they go beyond two words, the plaster of their intellect starts crumbling.

Sometimes, just a few words—two or three—can change someone's fate or leave another on the verge of despair. A doctor saying "I'm sorry" or "Congratulations" can define the line between life and death. A three-word text—"Salary is credited"— becomes the budget declaration of a hardworking soul's entire month. A girlfriend's "I love you" or "Need to talk to you"— these are all the milestones in the timeline of love.

There's a shortage of jobs; *daal* and *aata* might not be available, but data is in full supply. That's why everyone has started vomiting words on social media. Words have been rebranded as "content." Mass production is happening everywhere. And now, the biggest problem is disposal of this garbage. When the mind is overfilled, it erupts like an overflowing municipality dustbin left unattended—such is the stench that even walking past is unbearable. Humans have turned into walking trash cans!

The opportunity to say *do shabd* isn't granted to every *aere-gaere-naathu-khaere* (random person), sir! In every city, there exist a few selected speakers who are always invited to say *do shabd* on any topic, anywhere. Whether it's a condolence meet, an institutional function, an inauguration, or a seminar—these people are in high demand everywhere.

Now, this art of speaking *do shabd* also comes in two types. First: those who obtain the license to speak via generous donations. Second: those who, without spending a single penny, manage to sneak in through the backdoor with a wild-card entry. These are the ones who seem to have been born just to say *do shabd*. Wherever they spot a crowd of four people, their *do shabd* spontaneously tumble out.

Once, a gentleman took the stage and was invited to say *do shabd*. He went on to speak twenty-one thousand words. When asked the reason behind such a speech assault, he replied, "Bhaiya, I've donated [1] 21,000. Now if I'm not allowed to speak 21,000 words, then what's the point?"

As for me, my entire life runs on *do shabd*. For me, simple words like "Thank you" and "Please" are enough. Life goes on just fine with them.

You can hurt anyone, and anyone can hurt you. But you must always have two words in your pocket—just like an emergency fund—ready to use.

Just like everyone has their own version of Ram, everyone also has their own *do shabd*. Like:

For the politician: "Bhaiyo aur Behno" (Brothers and Sisters)

For the editor: "Khed hai" (We regret)

For the publisher: "Books didn't sell" and "Royalty went to hell"

For the writer: "Manuscript is lost"

For the wife: "Suno ji" (Listen, dear)

For the husband: "You're right"

For the lover: "Jaanu please"

For the girlfriend: "Shopping kab?" (When are we going shopping?)

For the officer: "Leave approval pending"

For the employee: "Sir, leave"

For the minister: "Treasury empty"

For the contractor: "Bill pending"

For the doctor: "Sorry"

For the actor: "Camera, roll, action"

For the singer: "Hello, hello, mic testing"

For the cricketer: "No ball"

For the bachelor: "Shaadi kab?" (When's the wedding?)

For the mother-in-law: "Kaisi bahu?" (How's the daughter-in-law?)

For the neighbor: "Chai feeki rakhna" (Keep the tea light)

For the teacher: "Homework kahaan?" (Where's the homework?)

We had the *misfortune* of inviting one such intellectual creature, known for saying *do shabd*.

We reached his home. Pressed the doorbell. The dog came to the gate and started saying his own *do shabd*. We didn't quite understand his language. Just then, the gentleman himself appeared. With a few gestures, he sent the dog away. The dog tucked in his *do shabd* along with his tail and retreated to a corner.

Sir offered a smile—just as stingy as his words—barely escaping from one corner of his mouth.

We entered. The interior of the drawing room instantly confirmed that everything living or non-living connected to him had to meet intellectual standards. On the wall were portraits of three or four ideal intellectuals, much like himself.

There were shelves lined with almost 50 books—his own, peeking from behind the glass. A few were lying face down on the center table, their titles in clear view. His glasses lay on top of the pile, as though tired of bearing the burden of so much wisdom.

His intense eyes, his posture on the sofa, his expression—everything screamed "intellectual." He had twisted his body in such a way that he wouldn't have to exert himself to fully face us. Perhaps his brilliance would've been too much for us to handle.

As soon as he learned that I was a new writer, he bluntly asked, "How many of my books have you read?"

I froze. I didn't even have the courage to ask which ones he had written—none had ever crossed my radar. A wave of guilt washed over me. How could I dare to call myself a writer without having read him?

I gestured to my companion, who handed over the invitation. We tried to leave immediately—before sir wasted any more words on insignificant beings like us. We had made it out, just in time.

The Constitution is in Danger

The usual hustle and bustle outside the city's well-known government hospital was there, but today, something felt different. This unusual buzz is often seen when some convicted politician or a VIP is admitted. But today, the crowd gathered for an unidentified injured man shocked everyone. It was truly a matter of intrigue.

Much like *Peepli Live*, this man too seemed promising enough to fetch the news channels a fantastic TRP boost and hand the politicians a brand-new issue to milk.

So, without building more suspense, let's come straight to the point. A blood-soaked man was found lying on the street, badly injured. Whether he was hit by someone and left there, or someone deliberately assaulted and dumped him, wasn't clear yet. The police had begun investigating, but the first priority was to get him to a hospital. A call was made to 108 Ambulance, and he was rushed to the government hospital.

The police were waiting for him to regain consciousness. As soon as he opened his eyes, he gave his name—**"Samvidhan" (Constitution).**

The moment he uttered that, everyone was stunned. The booming mics of TV channels and headline-hungry newspapers turned the whole incident into *Breaking News* within seconds.

The public, already uneasy with the ongoing narrative of *"Samvidhan khatre mein hai"* (the Constitution is in danger), suddenly became agitated. A section entangled in constitutional debates, political parties pounding their chests over constitutional crises, and the ever-shifting organizations that conveniently lean left or right—all those who routinely appear as protectors of the Constitution—immediately sprang into action.

Hearing again that *"Samvidhan khatre mein hai"*, hordes of self-declared *"Samvidhan bhakts"* (Constitution devotees) descended. *Eent se eent baja di*—they created mayhem. Rallies were staged, protests held, public property was vandalized, buses were torched, homes and shops were set on fire. Police retaliated with lathicharge. In short, they made sure to create exactly the kind of chaos expected when *"the Constitution is in danger."* Every possible method was employed to supposedly keep the Constitution "out of danger." What can one do? To protect the Constitution and keep it out of danger, these *Samvidhan bhakts* often feel compelled to resort to unconstitutional actions—by stepping out of the very Constitution they're trying to defend.

Until now, people only *heard* that *"the Constitution is in danger,"* but no one had actually seen it. Every time questions were raised, politicians gave vague and evasive answers.

Someone said, "There's no need to see the Constitution; it's in our pocket. We'll tell you its condition once we come to power." Another one said, "Let the endangered Constitution be. We'll write a new one that'll never be in danger."

But today, with the Constitution actually lying injured and hospitalized, the public rushed to see it with their own eyes.

Meanwhile, the government snapped into action. The police department was ordered to ensure full security around the Constitution. The hospital was cordoned off. No ordinary citizen was allowed inside.

The government feared that an opposition party worker might try to harm the Constitution or pull out its oxygen tube. The responsibility was theirs, and they promised that no matter how much budget it cost, they would "fix" the Constitution.

Every hour, a bulletin was issued from the hospital detailing the Constitution's condition: *"Critical, but stable."*

Opposition parties began to panic. Their worry was that if the Constitution recovered and was no longer in danger, they would lose their core political issue. On the other hand, even within the ruling party, there were differing opinions. Some leaders wanted the Constitution to be properly treated and restored to full health. Others felt it should be left as-is and a brand new Constitution should quietly be drafted in the background.

The Constitution lay there, eyes shut, on a hospital bed.

A parade of VIPs kept arriving. Each came encircled in security, visibly anxious, expressing concern—but it wasn't clear whether they feared losing their chairs or genuinely feared for the Constitution.

All the politicians kept repeating the same line over and over again:

"Samvidhan abhi bhi khatre mein hai..."

("The Constitution is still in danger...")

- Dr. Mukesh Aseemit

Email: drmukeshaseemit@gmail.com